untangle

Break Wrong Soul Ties
And Pursue Your Purpose

TERRI SAVELLE FOY

Published by Terri Savelle Foy Ministries
Rockwall, Texas, U.S.A.
www.terri.com
Printed in the U.S.A.

Scripture quotations are taken from the following:

ISBN 978-0-9854477-0-0

Rights for publishing this book outside the U.S.A. or in non-English languages are administered by Terri Savelle Foy Ministries, an international not-for-profit ministry. For additional information, please visit terri.com or, email info@terri.com, or write to
Terri Savelle Foy Ministries, PO Box 1959, Rockwall, TX 75087, U.S.A.

To order copies of this book and other resources in bulk quantities, please contact us at 1-877-661-8736.

My prayer is that this book will:

· Open your eyes to the truth if you're being deceived
· Save marriages, save callings, and save careers from being destroyed
· Provide the strength to end an unhealthy relationship
· Inspire vision to wake up tomorrow morning with a plan

CONTENTS

INTRODUCTION

The fact that you're reading this book reveals that a relationship has ended or needs to end. Just reading those words may bring pain to your heart all over again. By now, you probably know the numbing feeling of grieving a relationship. The feelings of hopelessness, being broken inside and not being able to see beyond today are all too common. Perhaps you're staring at the phone and hearing nothing. You're wondering if you should delete them as a friend on Facebook. Or should you just block their profile? Time is spent re-reading old texts again, and you are hurting in a way that you've never hurt before. I want you to know that you are not the only person to go through this. As a matter of fact, there are more than 3.19 million Google search results on the subject of "How to get over a break up".

I understand first-hand the pain and confusion that is associated with having negative soul ties. I've shared my story in other books and resources, but feel I should give you some background on my life as we get started. Growing up in a strong Christian family, no one would have guessed some of the things I went through. In my early teens, I was violated sexually by a stranger at a water park and never talked about it. I even thought it was my fault. Later, I was in an intimate relationship with a physically abusive boyfriend. I lived with a sense of shame, guilt, and a lack of self-worth. When all my friends told me to walk away from this ungodly relationship, I simply could not. I was tied to him in my soul. We had experienced so much together (good and bad). Besides, he said he would change. Soul ties are responsible for the pain we feel when a relationship ends. They are extremely powerful. Soul ties have deceived many young people looking for love, many married adults flirting with disaster, and many abused spouses trapped in a vicious cycle.

Let me also mention the topic of soul ties and marriage briefly here. If you are married to an unbeliever, I am in no way saying you need to leave your spouse and seek to break this soul tie. The Bible is clear regarding this. 1 Corinthians 7:12-13 addresses this very issue and says, "If any brother has a wife who is not a believer and she is willing to live with him, he must not divorce her. And if a woman has a husband who is not a believer and he is willing to live with her, she must not divorce him" (*NIV*). Being married to someone who does not want to follow God can be extremely difficult, but 1 Peter 3:1 gives the promise that the unbelieving spouse will be won over by the behavior of the believing spouse. However, let me be very clear; if your spouse is abusive, you need to get out of that environment as quickly as you can and seek help.

This book will address many questions and help you understand how soul ties are formed, how to recognize if you have wrong soul ties and how to break free once and for all. When you finish this book, you will not only be over the past, you will be on a pursuit! You can only conquer your past by focusing on your future. If you apply the practical steps outlined throughout this book, you will be a person with vision and a plan.

Chapter 1

The Body Language
of Flirting

One of the most memorable and exhilarating feelings in the world is getting into a relationship. For many, the best part is the leading up to it...the flirting.

Do you remember the High School Awards given to the *Most Flirtatious Girl* or *Most Flirtatious Boy*? Every girl hoped it wasn't her; every guy prayed it was him! Flirting is fun, exciting and it arouses curiosity about the one to whom you're giving this playful attention.

Flirting seems harmless. So, is it wrong to flirt if you're married? Or is it okay if it never goes beyond just that? The *Merriam Webster Dictionary* (2000) defines flirting as "to behave amorously without serious intent". If we go back even further, the *Thorndike-Barnhart 1968 Edition* reads: "making love without meaning it."

Flirting communicates a message whether you realize it or not (single or married). What is that message? Sexual or romantic interest in another person. If you are married and have no plans to have sexual or romantic interest in any one other than your spouse, then it would be wise to avoid this playful behavior.

Verbal and Non-verbal Communication

Verbal communication signs of flirting (that leave no room for guessing) include the famous (and ridiculous) pick-up lines:

- "If I could rearrange the alphabet, I would put U and I together."
- "Excuse me, but I think I dropped something. My jaw!"
- "Do you have a map? Because I just keep on getting lost in your eyes."
- "Is there an airport nearby or is that just my heart taking off?"
- "Your legs must be tired because you've been running through my mind all night."
- "You're so sweet, you're going to put Hershey's out of business!"
- "You don't need car keys to drive me crazy!"
- "Baby, you're like a student, and I'm like a math book. You solve all my problems."
- "I hope there's a fireman around, cause you're smokin'!"
- "Poof! I'm here. Now what are your other 2 wishes?"
- "Are you a parking ticket? Because you've got fine written all over you."
- "I know I'm not a grocery item, but I can tell when you're

checking me out!"

I love to read those pick-up lines out loud in my conferences as the the crowds laugh and finish the sentences for me! However, studies show that up to 93% of our communication is non-verbal. You are communicating constantly without ever opening your mouth. Your eye movement, hand gestures, posture, and facial expressions are doing the talking for you.

While earning my Communications degree from Texas Tech University, we studied body language intently and discovered that body expression usually prevails over words. Your eyes communicate messages more than any other part of the human anatomy.

Signals of flirting with our eyes include:
- Batting your eyelashes
- Smiling with your eyes ("smizing")
- Winking at someone across the room
- Intimidating with stares of seduction ("bedroom eyes")
- Looking someone up and down from head to toe and giving that little "twinkle" that provokes interest

You know the saying that your eyes are the gateway to your soul. Your soul is made up of your mind, your will and your emotions. Your mind encompasses what you think, what you want and how you feel.

> "Your life tends to go in the direction of your most dominating thoughts."

We know through research that whatever a person thinks about, with intense desire, will eventually show up in their lives. If you think about a slice of vanilla cake with pink buttercream icing long enough, you will eventually have what you desire in your hands even if you have to drive to the store to make that happen! Napoleon Hill said, "Our brains become magnetized with the dominating thoughts we hold in our minds." In other words, your life tends to go in the direction of your most dominating thoughts. Whatever has your attention, eventually has your heart.

If a flirtatious glance from across the room is reciprocated, you can count on the fact that you will be thinking about it all day long. Whatever you think about, expands. If a woman gently touches a man's arm during a conversation and he thinks about that touch all night long, eventually, thoughts will lead to actions. There will come a time when thinking about her is no longer enough. I heard someone say, "Where the mind goes, the man follows." We simply follow our thoughts.

Many married people flirt out of curiosity, loneliness and perhaps feeling of passion and attractiveness again. Flirting could be a means to do mentally what you *think* you would never do physically. Think again. It has been proven time and again, everything gets its start in the mind. Plenty of divorced people say flirting with others slowly led to adultery which ruined their marriage. Where did the flirting start? In their mind.

10 common signs revealing that you are flirting with the opposite sex:

Playing with hair. Women who move their hands through their hair display a message of feeling attractive. Allowing hair to cover one side of the face and one eye reveals a seductive look that you could be giving off.

Raised eyebrows. When men/women find someone of the opposite sex attractive, they tend to raise their eyebrows in a positive sign of interest.

Eye contact. It's obvious there is definite interest when you make eye contact with the opposite sex and hold it for a significant amount of time. Regularly glancing at someone from across the room is a strong sign of flirting.

Giggling. When you laugh at the dumbest jokes and everything they say is somehow hilarious, it's a clear sign to them and to everyone around you that you are flirting.

Leaning towards him/her. This physical sign of body language reveals that he/she wants to be closer to you. Be aware if they are leaning into you or away from you. Both speak volumes.

Playing with accessories. Women who twirl their necklaces, twist their earrings or spin their ring around their finger are giving off signs of "shy-girl" flirting. Men tend to play with the change in their pockets as a nervous sign of flirting.

Dressing up. Are you experimenting with new looks, adding more make-up, changing your style of clothing and constantly aware of how you look? Others are noticing these changes in you, too.

Lowered head/looking up. Otherwise known as giving "bedroom eyes". This form of body language is very bold and seductive and leaves no room for confusion. You are flirting!

Looking at lips. When you're attracted to someone, you could be subconsciously focusing on their lips giving the clear sign, "I wonder what it would be like to kiss you."

Physical touch. Lightly touching someone's arm or slightly hitting them on the shoulder can show a sign of playful flirting. It's a nonverbal sign that you're open and friendly.

There are many forms of touch that are blatant, outspoken, clear signs of interest, but be aware of the subtle touches implying the same message.

Life at 20%

Yes, it's fun to read about flirting and see if you are exercising any of these flirt tactics consciously or unconsciously. I'm not saying that it's a sin to ever think about the opposite sex. Everyone is tempted to do that. I am saying to be careful what you think.

"Your thoughts will be the pathway to your destiny."
– T. D. Jakes

If you're thinking about someone *that you don't need to be thinking about*, it's just a matter of time and you will be with that person in a way that leads to much, much regret.

You might ask, "What's so wrong with flirting with a little sin?" A little sin is like being a little pregnant. Eventually, it will reveal itself. Whatever gets in your mind and stays there will eventually show up in your life. Or you could say *whoever* is on your mind and stays there will eventually show up in your life.

Attaching yourself to wrong soul ties can lead you to:
· Destroy your marriage

- Lose the respect of your children
- Forfeit the plan of God for your life
- Feel dirty, used, sleazy, worthless, or insecure
- Feel bound to stay with someone because of what you've done with them
- Have deep feelings of regret

I heard T.D. Jakes describe life using an 80/20 principle. He said that the most we will ever experience in life is about 80%. The best life for most of us will be living at 80%. However, your enemy, Satan, will present 20% to you and say, "This is what you're missing. Wouldn't life be complete if you had this 20%? This is the only thing missing in your life. How can you go your entire life without experiencing this 20%?"

He will do his best to convince you that you cannot live without this 20% until you're willing to give up the 80% you have for the 20% you don't have. Then look at what you're left with: 20%. That's what wrong soul ties will produce. Life at 20%.

If you're being tempted to flirt with this 20% right now, then it's a divine appointment that you are reading this today. God wants you to wake up! Enjoy and embrace the 80% you already have. God can make up the difference.

You may be entangled with 20% right now, and you're miserable inside. Open your eyes and see the trap. I'm going to walk you through this process of breaking wrong soul ties and gaining the freedom to move on with your life.

Read this personal note from God to you:

"The Lord is my constant companion.
There is no need that He cannot fulfill.
Whether His course for me points
    to the mountaintops of glorious joy
    or to the valleys of human suffering,
He is by my side.
He is ever present with me.
He is close beside me, when I tread the dark streets of danger,
    even when I flirt with death itself, He will not leave me.
When the pain is severe,
    He is near to comfort.
When the burden is heavy,

He is there to lean upon.

When depression darkens my soul,

He touches me with eternal joy.

When I feel empty and alone,

He fills the aching vacuum with His power.

My security is in His promise

to be near me always

and in the knowledgement that He will never let me go!"

Psalm 23 (Psalms Now)

God loves you. He will *never* let you go!

I want you to grab hold of this promise from God Himself to you. God is not mad at you. He loves you just as much today as He always has. His love is not dependent upon your past performances. He loves you because He is love. God and all of Heaven are cheering you on, hoping that you will wake up and embrace the joyous life He still has prearranged for you.

> "Life is not over because the relationship is."

When you close this book, you will have a plan. The plan I'm going to unfold for you is something I have walked out in my own life, and it has empowered me to live my dreams and never look back. Trust me, you're going to smile again. You're going to sleep peacefully again. You're going to breathe again. You're going to dream bigger than before.

Life is not over because the relationship is. There is so much life for you to enjoy.

"Thank you for this message. I got it at a time when I was so tempted to commit adultery with an ex-boyfriend. I am a Pastor's wife and mom of three. I am also completing my Masters degree at college. I usually meet this guy at college and that is how the temptation began.

He is in a very troubled marriage and I thought that by maintaining communication with him, that I could help him. I really felt for him and wanted him to get closer to God so that the Lord could heal his marriage.

Anyways, what actually happened is that we started to get emotionally entangled and although nothing happened in the physical, it became an emotional type of adultery.

When I heard this message from you, I felt as if you knew me and was talking directly to me. It sobered me up to realize that I am in a war and that Satan hates me and has devised plans for my downfall. Your message has given me the strength to cut off all communication with him and just pray for his marriage from a 'safe distance' rather than direct communication with him.

It has been almost two months now since I made that decision and I feel so light and relieved and have learned a valuable lesson from that experience."

- Grateful Sister

Chapter 2

Four Indicators of
Wrong Soul Ties

Out of the hundreds of video podcasts I've recorded, my highest viewed videos on YouTube are on "Breaking Soul Ties". I receive countless emails, letters and messages from women and men with questions about this intimate topic. They've had adulterous affairs and don't know how to break free from that person. They admit that it's wrong, but cannot seem to get them out of their mind. Teenagers have crossed the line with various partners and don't know how to make things right. Old flames have rekindled an inappropriate secret romance. They grieve in their soul when that person rejects them, moves on to someone else, or God clearly instructs them to end things. To put it mildly, soul ties are powerful.

What Are Soul Ties?

A *soul tie is an emotional bond or connection that unites you with someone else*. You can literally become chained or bound to a person through your soul. Again, your soul is made up of your mind, your will and your emotions. It comprises what you think, what you want and how you feel.

Have you found yourself tormented by thoughts about a person, excessively wondering about them, checking on them, rehearsing times with them? You have soul ties. Have you grieved over a severed relationship with someone you were once close to? You have soul ties. Do you miss them, long for them, desire to be with them? You have soul ties.

Not all soul ties are bad. You can have good soul ties with your spouse, your parents, your siblings, your closest friends, your co-workers, your teammates, your roommates, your care group, etc. God wants us to have healthy relationships that build us up, provides wisdom, and gives godly counsel.

> *"When David had finished speaking to Saul, the soul of Jonathan was knit with the soul of David, and Jonathan loved him as his own life"* (1 Sam. 18:1, AMP).

Soul ties are formed through close friendships, through vows, commitments and promises, and through physical intimacy. God will strategically bring good relationships into our lives to form healthy soul ties. In contrast, Satan always brings *counterfeits* into our lives to form unhealthy soul ties. What is a counterfeit? By definition, it is something made in exact imitation of something valuable or important with the intention to deceive or defraud. That's exactly how your enemy, Satan, operates . . . through deception.

There are several ways unhealthy soul ties are formed including:
- Abusive relationships (physically, sexually, emotionally, verbally)
- Adulterous affairs
- Sex before marriage
- Obsessive entanglements with a person (giving them more authority in your life than you give to God)
- Controlling relationships
- And many other ways

When soul ties are good and healthy, the power of God is magnified. Matthew 18:19 says, "If two of you shall agree on earth as touching any thing that they shall ask, it shall be done for them" (*KJV*). There are evident emotions of love, peace and contentment in healthy soul tie relationships.

On the contrast, when soul ties are bad and unhealthy, the power of Satan is magnified. I believe there are clear indicators when wrong soul ties have been formed and should be recognized and respected.

Four Indicators of Wrong Soul Ties:

1. Confusion

2. Misery

3. Torment

4. Disobedience to God

1. *"I feel so confused."*

When you are outside the will of God in a particular relationship, you are simply confused. Your feelings tell you one thing; your spirit tells you another. You want to believe your feelings because they seem so real and seem to scream the loudest, but something deep inside of you tells you differently. That's where the confusion comes in.

What is confusion? *It is a lack of proper order and being mentally "mixed up".* Confusion is caused by mixing darkness with light.

"God is not the author of confusion but of peace" (1 Cor. 14:33, *KJV*).

If you are not experiencing peace in this relationship or "soul tie", then something is not right. That is the Holy Spirit warning you and working to get your attention. The Holy Spirit will actually withdraw our peace when we are outside of God's will. That gut feeling that you have could be the Holy Spirit telling you to get out of this relationship now.

Galatians 1:7 says, "Evidently some people are throwing you into confusion and are trying to pervert the Gospel of Christ" (*NIV*). You need to respect these warnings. They are not to be brushed off or treated as a small thing. Honor the Holy Spirit's leading in your life. You should not feel confused if you are in the will of God, and honestly, why would you want to be any other place?

When you are confused about a relationship, you can make unwise, regretful decisions. You need to take purposeful steps in feeding your spirit the truth of God's Word. The truth always overrides deception.

As you begin to seek God for clarity and wisdom, start by simply lifting your hands to heaven and worshiping God. Why? Worship and praise invites the very presence of God into your home, your car, your office, your bedroom or wherever you are. Confusion cannot coexist in the presence of God. Psalm 22:3 tells us that God inhabits the praises of

His people.

2. "I'm just miserable."

As long as we are actively sinning against God, we will stay miserable. As Joyce Meyer puts it, "There's nothing more miserable than a born again sinner." When we persist in doing something that we know God is not in agreement with, we will experience a type of misery that doesn't go away.

What is misery? It is *a state or feeling of great distress or discomfort of mind or body*. You may feel uneasy inside, extreme anxiety, sorrow or pain. You may literally feel disgusted by what you're doing, yet you feel powerless to change your situation. Those are all indicators that Satan is at work in your life to destroy it.

You can repent now and ask God to forgive you for any entanglements with a wrong soul tie that has produced misery in your soul. David cried out in Psalm 38:8, "I am exhausted and completely crushed. My groans come from an anguished heart." (*NLT*). Does that describe how you feel when you're alone? There is hope.

Psalm 23:3 says, "He restores my soul" (*NIV*). Those four little words will redefine your life. God will restore your mind, your will and your emotions. Memorize that scripture and speak it out of your mouth every time misery invades your soul. Say it right now, "Thank you, Lord, for restoring my soul."

Remember the phrase "misery loves company"? That is true when it comes to justifying wrong soul ties. If the only time you feel "okay" about this relationship is when you're with them—misery loves company. Don't justify what your conscience condemns. Obey the Holy Spirit and don't make regrets.

3. *"My mind is tormented."*

A tormented mind is not the mind of Christ. The mind of Christ is one that is at peace no matter what the circumstances. When Satan has invaded our souls through wrong soul ties, our minds *will not* be at rest. This is where your battle will take place. Period.

Do you feel exhausted, empty, uneasy, sad, depressed, lonely or hopeless? Then the Evil One has been given too much access to your mind.

Is your mind *constantly* replaying images of the past and rehearsing previous conversations like a broken record? Do your thoughts produce fear or make you feel unclean? Whatever is going on in your mind is affecting your emotional state.

Your feelings are indicators of what you are thinking about. If you feel depressed, then you are thinking depressing thoughts. If you feel ashamed, then you are thinking shame-filled thoughts.

2 Corinthians 10:5 says that we are to renew our minds by taking "captive every thought to make it obedient to Christ" (*NIV*). I will be the first to admit that this is not easy, but it is necessary. You *can* do this. As a Christian you can get your thoughts under the control of your reborn spirit. How? By speaking God's Word out of your mouth every single time a negative thought enters your mind.

"You've got to be kidding me, Terri!" No, I'm not. You cannot defeat thoughts with thoughts. You defeat thoughts with words. When I learned this powerful key, it caused me to make giant strides in my path to victory.

> Say it right now, "Thank you, Lord, for restoring my soul."

For example, let's say I asked you to recite the alphabet in your head. As you get about half way through the letters, I interrupt you and ask you to give me directions to your house. Your mind would have to stop thinking of the alphabet in order to hear what your mouth is speaking with directions. It works the same way with defeating a tormented mind by speaking God's Word out of your mouth.

Every time those debilitating thoughts enter your mind, speak a scripture out loud. *Don't just think it, speak it.* It can be as simple as saying: "Thank You, Lord, that you restore my soul"…over and over and over.

My favorite scripture is: "Lord, I do not remember the former things, nor consider the things of old; behold, you are doing a new thing in my life and *now* it shall spring forth" (I personalized Isaiah 43:18-19).

Be persistent. There's nothing Satan hates more than to hear you speak the Word of God and the name of Jesus out of your mouth!

4. *"I didn't mean to disobey God...on purpose."*

You may not actively or consciously choose to disobey God. However, when you don't do what He's telling you to do, you've disobeyed. According to Deuteronomy, obedience opens the doors for God's blessings on our lives; disobedience opens the door for a curse on our lives (Deuteronomy 28).

If you feel like you have been dealing with this situation for far too long and nothing seems to help you get beyond it, remember this phrase: *God will not advance your instructions beyond your last act of disobedience.*

If you don't fully obey what God is telling you to do, you will never move beyond your current circumstances. I don't know what that means to you, but I know what it meant for me years ago. I was desperate to move beyond my circumstances no matter how painful it would be.

Why would we disobey God?
· We doubt our ability to hear from God
· It's hard
· It hurts too badly
· It's uncomfortable
· It's not what our flesh "wants" to do
· We say that we are waiting for God to change us
· We are waiting for God to change someone else

I believe we try to find answers to our problems that won't make us uncomfortable. We are waiting for something easier, but we stay miserable inside.

What is God telling you to do? Be honest with yourself right now. If God was standing in front of you right now, what do you believe He would instruct you to do in your situation?

> You will never regret obeying God. *Never.*

What did God tell you to do in the past, but you didn't do it because it felt too difficult? And here it is a year later and you're still struggling.

Remember, *partial obedience is still disobedience.* Delayed obedience is still disobedience. And disobedience keeps us under a curse. You will be miserable. Do what God is telling you to do knowing ahead of time that it's always for your benefit. God is not trying to hurt you. He's trying to help you. He sees what you don't see.

Stormie Omartian says, "The more obedient you are, the more bondage will be stripped away from your life. There is also a certain healthy confidence that comes from knowing you've obeyed God."

Your obedience is a reflection of your love for God. John 14:15 says, "If you really love Me, you will obey" (*AMP*). You will never regret obeying God. Never. As you continue reading and opening your heart up to hear the truth, I am going to give you some practical action steps to keep you focused on where you're headed and not what you're leaving.

Chained and trapped by wrong soul ties for 43 years!

"Precious sister, Terri! I am now sixty-nine years of age, been a spirit-filled Christian, and an ordained minister of the gospel since 1980. I have traveled in an evangelistic/prophetic ministry of my own for nearly 20 years, but have been so very miserable and bound up, stuck, chained and trapped by Satan's plan by being tied to my ex for over 43 years! Yes, that's right! I divorced him FOUR times, Terri, and kept going back to him. I am still with him because I have no other place to live except in our house!

I've tried to get free from him but he would not leave me alone and I FOOLISHLY believed his lies, even after leaving him all those times. Now I am sixty-nine and am dying inside because when one is truly called of God for ministry, and I am, they are totally miserable, which I have been all these years, and still am! Yes, soul ties!

I led all four of my children to the Lord and into the baptism of the Holy Spirit way back in the 70's, even my ex. But he never wanted to read or study the Bible, when I could not put it down. Many souls were saved, and many signs, wonders and miracles happened through my ministry, Terri, and that is my deepest heart's desire…to serve my Lord Jesus till His return. I've been so robbed through these soul ties!

I am believing for my supernatural breakthrough. And breaking soul ties with this man, and many men and people in my life, is the new beginning God desired for me to take. The words you've used in this soul ties message is exactly what my life has been like. NO MORE! I am on the path of my new beginning, starting NOW! My Exodus is NOW! I know God has a marvelous plan, purpose and destiny yet for me to fulfill, and I am on my way! And thank you, Terri! God bless you and your family. I love you!"

-LaVonne

Chapter 3

When Soul Ties
Go Wrong

Statistics have shown that approximately one in three women is beaten, coerced into having sex or otherwise abused at some stage during their lives. Other statistics indicate that domestic violence is still the single biggest threat of injury to women—more than cancer, heart attacks, strokes, muggings, car accidents and rapes combined! Sadly, one online site stated that the most dangerous place for a woman is in her own home.

Abusive Soul Ties

Are you in an abusive relationship? Are you in denial about being in an abusive relationship? I know I was. In my college years, I became entangled in an intimate relationship with someone who was so possessive of me and threw wild fits of jealousy and rage if I even looked at another guy.

Looking from the outside in, you would assume that as a young, popular, Christian girl I would instantly jump as far as I could from a guy who would even think about choking me, banging my head against the steering wheel of a car or dragging me by my neck through a parking lot. But I didn't. I forgave. I stayed with him. Why? Soul ties.

I remember sitting in my dorm room with my roommate one afternoon between classes and watching Geraldo Rivera. The topic of the day was "Teens in abusive relationships". I watched it and felt so sorry for those girls. I could not understand why they didn't just wake up and run! *Get away from that jerk! Who does he think he is to hit them, strangle them, and intimidate them with anger!* I naively thought this as I watched a mirror image of myself.

I sat there in complete denial that I was one of them.

Abusive people have a unique ability to distort our perception of what is really happening and even about what is right and wrong. We begin to doubt our own feelings so much that we can't make wise decisions.

"Make no friendship with an angry man; and with a furious man do not go: otherwise you'll learn his ways and get a snare in your soul" (Prov. 22:24-25, *NKJV*).

A snare is a trap. You can become so trapped in this relationship that you don't even see a way out. I couldn't. As much as I hated what he was doing and at times hated him for it, I still could not imagine him with another girl. I could not imagine leaving him for good, not after what we had shared. That's the trap.

"Don't befriend angry people or associate with hot-tempered people, or you will learn to be like them and endanger your soul." (Prov. 22:24-25, *NLT*).

The Message translation says it this way, "Don't hang out with angry people; don't keep company with hotheads. Bad temper is contagious—don't get infected."

Some clear signs that you may be in an abusive relationship, if he/she:
- Is highly possessive of you
- Is irrationally jealous
- Is violent with you
- Has fits of rage and uncontrolled temper
- Isolates you from friendships and family relationships
- Controls you and your whereabouts
- Has a history of abusive or bad relationships
- Places responsibility for their out of control behavior on you

· Scares or intimidates you
· Causes you to fear ending the relationship even though you
   know it's the right thing to do
· Forces you to perform sexual acts

Many abusive partners will constantly keep track of your time, accuse you of being unfaithful for no reason, accuse you of flirting, criticize or belittle you—which are all major signs of insecurity within themselves. Often times, friends and family recognize abnormal behavior and warn us. Therefore, the abuser will discourage your relationships with friends and family for fear of you listening to their life-saving advice.

You need to hear from God. He will always provide the wisdom and guidance you need. You are valuable to God. Your body is valuable. Your opinions are valuable. God doesn't want His precious child being mistreated. Cry out to Him. Psalm 118:5 says, "In my anguish I cried to the Lord, and he answered by setting me free" (*NIV*).

Sexual Soul Ties

In our desperate need for love and affection, approval and closeness, many of us find ourselves falling into the arms of the wrong person. The more intimate you are with someone, the stronger that bond becomes. Sexual immorality is having sex with anyone to whom you are not married. God is not trying to withhold good from us by instructing us to withfrain from sex outside of marriage. He has developed certain guidelines for *our benefit.*

Having sexual intercourse isn't just a physical encounter, it invades our soul. That's why God's instructions for when we are facing sexual temptation are very clear: *flee* (1 Cor. 6:18).

There's a reason God commanded us to run for our lives from this temptation. The road to recovery from sexual sin seems to be the most painful and requires the longest amount of healing time. "He who commits sexual immorality sins against his own body" (1 Cor. 6:18, *NKJV*).

God's original plan was for a man and woman to unite sexually as marriage partners. He wants us to have soul ties with our spouse. "For 'the two', He says, 'shall become one flesh'" (1 Cor. 6:16, *NKJV*).

Once you have given yourself to someone sexually, the Bible says you become one. If you are not married, and that person is not obligated to be faithful to you or the relationship has ended, your soul may feel as if it is being ripped apart.

Consequences to Casual Sex

> Having sexual intercourse isn't just a physical encounter, it invades our soul.

There really are consequences to casually sleeping around. Therapists call it "emotional anorexia" or learning to survive without relationships. It is damaging to your self-esteem and generates deep feelings of rejection whether you admit it or not.

According to PhysiciansForLife.org, there are 10 negative psychological effects of sex outside of marriage (for teens and adults):

1. Worry about pregnancy and STDs

Teens are worried and distracted each month that they might be pregnant. Girls often buy home pregnancy kits and have a great deal of anxiety in their day-to-day activities.

2. Regret and self-recrimination

"I get upset when I see my friends losing their virginity to some guy they've just met. Later, after the guys dumped them, they come to me and say, 'I wish I hadn't done it.'"

A ninth-grade girl who slept with eight boys in junior high says, "I'm young, but I feel old." Girls are more likely to see sex as a sign of commitment in the relationship. They often feel cheap and cheated.

"I never imagined I'd pay so dearly and for so long. Sex without commitment is very risky for the heart," says a 33-year-old psychiatrist from personal experience.

3. Guilt

Guilt is a special form of regret; it is a strong sense of having done something morally wrong. Morality refers to a code of behavior.

Guilt is a normal and healthy moral response, a sign that one's conscience is working. Guilt may come from seeing the hurt that one has caused other people by using them as sex objects. Guilt may come from knowing your parents would be upset if they knew of your sexual involvement.

Guilt about sexual pasts can cripple people when they do get married through flashbacks of previous sexual experiences.

4. Loss of self-respect and self-esteem

Many people suffer loss of self-respect when they discover they have a sexually transmitted disease. Most people have no idea how prevalent STDs are. When they become infected themselves, they feel very "dirty".

Even without STD infection, temporary sexual relationships can lower the self-respect of both the user and the used. Casual sex can lower self-esteem, which leads a person into further casual sex, which leads to further loss of self-esteem in an oppressive cycle, which is hard to break.

5. The corruption of character and the debasement of sex

When people treat others as sexual objects and exploit them for their own pleasure, they not only lose self-respect, they corrupt their characters and debase their sexuality in the process. Good character consists of virtues such as respect, responsibility, honesty, fairness, caring, and self-control.

With regard to sex, self-control is particularly crucial. The breakdown of sexual self-control is a big factor in many of the sex-related problems that plague our society: rape, promiscuity, pornography, sexual harassment, sexual abuse of children, sexual infidelity in marriage, and more.

6. Shaken trust and fear of commitment

Young people who feel used or betrayed after the break-up of a sexual relationship may experience difficulty in future relationships. Some develop a low self-esteem and they seek any type of attention, no matter how short-lived and demeaning; others withdraw and have trouble trusting any more.

One young woman noted: "Besides feeling cheap (after several sexual relationships), I began to wonder if there would ever be anyone who would love and accept me without demanding that I do something with my body to 'earn' that love."

Boys also experience loss of trust: "I'm afraid of falling in love."

7. Rage over betrayal

Sometimes the emotional reaction to being "dumped" isn't just a lack of trust or fear of commitment, but rage. The sense of betrayal is usually much greater if sex has been part of the relationship. Sex can be emotional dynamite.

8. Depression and suicide

Sometimes the rupture of relationships leads to deep depression that may lead, in turn, to suicide. In the past 25 years, teen suicide has tripled. In a 1988 survey by the U.S. Department of Health and Human Services, 1 of 5 adolescent girls stated they had tried to kill themselves (1 of 10 for boys).

9. Ruined relationships

Sex can cause another kind of emotional consequence by turning good relationships bad. Other dimensions of the relationship stop developing and negative emotions enter, such as anger, impatience, jealousy, and selfishness.

10. Stunting personal development

Premature sexual involvement can not only stunt the development of the relationship, it can also stunt one's development as a person. Some young people handle anxieties by turning to drugs and alcohol, while others turn to sex.

Sex is most joyful and fulfilling—most emotionally and physically safe, when it occurs within a loving, total, and binding life-long commitment, historically called marriage.

(Used by permission from PhysiciansForLife.Org)

I would like to add an 11th point to these consequences of casual sex:

11. Separation from God

Isaiah 59:1-2 says, "Surely the arm of the Lord is not too short to save, nor his ear too dull to hear. But your iniquities have *separated you from your God;* your sins have hidden his face from you, so that he will not hear" (*NIV*, emphasis added).

God is a forgiving God and a loving Heavenly Father; however, sin separates us from Him. When we *remain* in *willful* disobedience to God, a wall goes up between us. That's not a place any of us want to be.

Hebrews 10:26 says, "For if we sin willfully after we have received the knowledge of the truth, there no longer remains a sacrifice for sins" (*NKJV*).

Sometimes we need this wake up call to stop doing what we are doing. We can't justify it any longer. God is not pleased when we willfully continue in sin. There are consequences too big to pay.

I want you to be brutally honest with yourself if you are engaging in premarital sex or sex outside of marriage and recognize the urgency to stop. Ask the Lord to forgive you. Do not be too ashamed to go to Him. He already knows. Let the tears flow. Get in His presence and confess it to Him.

Sin destroys our lives. We must get it out of us. Whether you initiated it or not. Whether you intended to or not. Release it from your life now. Ask the Lord to forgive you and to remove this residue of sin from your life. If you fall again, don't let it stop you from going to God. He is not mad at you. He is the only One who can truly give you the supernatural strength to resist and be free.

If you have a strong sexual addiction, then you may need to seek counseling. Do not withdraw from God. Lean on Him like never before. Do not justify sexual behavior because you've already yielded to it. It's never too late to start over, be cleansed, and feel pure.

If you feel as if a sexual relationship has caused you to feel chained to this person and you cannot seem to break free, read this scripture out loud:

"Then they cried out to the Lord in their trouble, and He saved them out of their distresses. He brought them out of darkness

and the shadow of death, and broke their chains in pieces" (Ps. 107:13-14, *NKJV*).

God promises to deliver those who cry out to Him. The moment you cry out, He comes running. God is a gentleman; He waits for you to call on Him.

"The righteous cry out and the Lord hears them; he delivers them from all their troubles. The Lord is close to the broken-hearted and saves those who are crushed in spirit" (Ps. 34:17-18, *NIV*).

That's the God you serve. That's His desire for you, to heal you everywhere you hurt.

God is a gentleman; He waits for you to call on Him.

"Tried and tried to break it off...but kept giving in"

"I had been a virgin for 39 years of my life and a few years ago that ended with my ex-boyfriend. The intimate relationship had gone on for almost a year and a half and I knew it was wrong. Through that time period I tried and tried to break it off (the intimacy)…sometimes abstaining from it, but weeks later he would initiate contact and even though I still knew it wasn't right, I'd give in. As of 3 months ago, I have officially broken up with him because I value myself more than he does. Since breaking up, thoughts of him come across my mind from time to time and I now understand it's because of intimate soul ties. I couldn't sleep much on one particular night because I constantly thought about him to the point I had to get up and pray in the spirit. I also searched the internet to find this message from you. I will definitely plan to get your book. I want these thoughts and images of him completely buried forever."

-Kim

Chapter 4

The Morning After

Every year, businesses spend billions of dollars creating catchy jingles and memorable slogans all in an attempt to convince us to buy what they are selling. See if you can connect the slogans with the right company to these unforgettable advertising campaigns through the years:

1. "Because I'm worth it."

2. "Don't leave home without it."

3. "When it absolutely, positively has to be there overnight."

4. "Have it your way."

5. "The quicker picker upper."

6. "Reach out and touch someone."

7. "Finger lickin' good."

8. "I'm lovin' it."

9. "Good to the last drop."

10. "Where's the beef?"

A. AT&T

B. McDonald's

C. Maxwell House

D. KFC

E. Wendy's

F. L'Oreal

G. Burger King

H. American Express

I. Federal Express

J. Bounty Paper Towels

How many did you get right? If you were fairly successful, this means that they *got your attention*. After all, that's what they are after: your attention. Advertising agents realize that whatever gets in your mind and stays there will eventually show up in your life. This is especially true concerning former relationships.

Your attention is a powerful thing. Attention is defined as *notice taken of someone or something; the regarding of someone or something as interesting or important; the mental faculty of considering or taking notice of someone or something.*

Albert Einstein said, "Your imagination is everything. It's simply a preview of life's coming attractions." In other words, whatever has your attention, you are attracting in your life.

Advertising Agent

So the question is: exactly what is in your mind? What are you imagining? You have an enemy, Satan, who is fighting for your attention. He wants you tormented by your past. He wants you dwelling on old memories of that person, longing for them, aching inside and re-living each encounter. He knows that if he can get ungodly cravings to grab your attention, your life will veer off in that direction. Therefore, he has become an "advertising agent" fighting for your attention.

The top 10 "power words" in advertising according to the psychology department at Yale University are (from eBizine: An eBrand Media Publication):

10. New – It's part of basic human makeup to seek novelty

9. Save – We all want to save something

8. Safety – This could refer to health or long-lasting quality

7. Proven – Helps remove fear from trying something new

6. Love – Continues to be an all-time favorite

5. Discover – Presents a sense of excitement and adventure

4. Guarantee – Provides a sense of safety at the time of purchase

3. Health – Especially powerful when it applies to a product

2. Results – Works in rationalizing a purchase

1. You – Listed as the #1 most powerful word in every study reviewed

Because of the personal nature of advertising copywriting, you should always use "you" in your headline, opening line and as often as possible. In fact, many copywriters will throw out a headline if "you" is not in it.

The "advertising agent," Satan, specializes in crafting sentences that appeal to your vulnerabilities. Why? He wants your undivided attention. He wants you distracted from the original purpose and plan God crafted for your life. He wants to divert your attention through very creative advertising.

"This *new* relationship will save you from loneliness and bring you the safety and security you're longing for," he tells the married man or woman.

"He has *proven* to love you like no one else. It's okay to sleep with him," he whispers to the teenage girl.

"*Discover* the possibilities," he advertises to the college student tempted to have a one-night-stand.

"I *guarantee* you will be happier than ever," he seductively convinces the unhappy man considering divorce.

"This affair won't affect your *health*," he tells the lady caught up in the excitement of being noticed by a married man.

"*You* can trust your feelings," he says to the depressed housewife on the verge of leaving.

The "advertising agent," Satan, specializes in crafting sentences that appeal to your vulnerabilities.

Satan whispers all the top-selling words in your ears. Why? He wants your attention. He wants to alter the direction of your life because he knows that whatever has your attention affects your direction. So what does he do? He must find an alternative craving to present to you.

The Bait

My husband, Rodney, loves to fish. On our annual vacations, he always takes one day to go on a chartered boat and just fish, while I do what I love to do—nothing. I want to just lay by the pool. I jokingly call him

"Fishing Rod". He has fished in some of the most spectacular world-class fishing spots across the globe. He has fished for Blue Marlin in Kona, Hawaii; Salmon in Alaska; Tuna in Australia; Trout in Montana and Catfish in our backyard pond!

I noticed with each type of fish he is trying to catch, he uses different bait. How does he know which bait to use on a Bass or a Trout? He tests it. He has tested many different lures over time to see which fish is "lured" by which bait. Once he discovers what appeals to each specific fish, he makes note of it. "Use minnows for a Bass. Use spinnerbaits for trout."

Then, he baits the hook with the lure that *appeals* to the fish he has his eye on. His goal is to disguise the hook so well that only the alluring bait is visible. He dangles that bait in front of that Catfish over and over and over. The Catfish may not fall for it right away; he knows that. He is prepared to be patient. It may take time.

He may go back another day and dangle that bait at the exact time of hunger. He knows that, too. He knows *when* to go after that fish. It could be as early as 5:00 A.M. Pretty soon, the Catfish is lured by the very bait that appeals to him the most. But what that fish doesn't realize is that on the other end of that delicious bait is a hook. That hook is designed with one intention: to kill him. Notice again: the *very thing* that lures him is the *very thing* that destroys him.

Satan works the same way with you. He knows exactly which "bait" appeals to you the most. His "bait" is designed with one intention: to kill, to steal and to destroy our lives.

"The thief comes only to steal and kill and destroy" (John 10:10, *NIV*).

Remember, he must identify a weakness in your flesh in order to draw your attention. How? He tests you. He brings things little by little to see what you'll fall for and what you will resist. He knows to bring *someone* that *lures* you, appeals to you and *captures* your attention or else you won't fall. It could be:

· Someone who caught your eye as very attractive
· Someone you miss
· Someone you loved at one time
· Someone who makes you feel better
· Someone who gives you attention and compliments
· Someone you were intimate with in the past

· Someone you were married to

James 1:14-16 warns us: "We are tempted when we are drawn away and *trapped* by our own evil desires. Then our evil desires conceive and give birth to sin; and sin, when it is full-grown, gives birth to death. Do not be deceived, my dear friends" (*GNT*).

The *Amplified* version reads this way: "…each one is tempted when he is drawn away, enticed and *baited* by his own evil desire."

Other translations use the word "lured": "…as he is beguiled *and lured…*" (*Moffatt*) "…when he is *lured* and enticed…" (*RSV*)

Think about that. The very thing that lured you leads to your death. Just like James said, "when sin is full-grown, gives birth to death."

I've heard Mac Hammond explain it this way. "You can choose life or you can choose death. If you choose to live by your flesh and what your flesh demands and desires, you're choosing death. And death will be manifest *all* around you." I interpret that as: the death of your marriage, the death of your health, the death of your career, the death of your family unit, the death of your confidence, the death of your finances as they are right now. Death is the result when we give our attention to what Satan is dangling in front of us, those temptations that are screaming so loud in our ears.

Satan has a unique way of keeping us so focused on the bait, giving it our full attention, that we don't even see the hook. I want you to see the big picture of your life. For a moment, step out of the day-to-day struggles and your feelings for this person, and look at the big picture.

Who has your attention right now?

Who are you spending the most time thinking about?

Is it healthy or unhealthy?

Is it selfish or unselfish?

Is it godly or ungodly?

Is it leading you into God's plan or away from God's plan?

If your attention is wrapped up primarily in thoughts that are un-healthy, selfish and ungodly, it's a trap. It's a counterfeit to God's plan. Don't fall for Satan's tricks. Don't fall for his traps that are tailor-made to destroy your life.

If you're in a situation right now where you are being tempted to do something that you know deep in your heart is not in line with God's plan for your life in fact, you flat out know it's wrong—*don't do it*!

I do not believe it is a coincidence that you are reading this book at this very moment. God is warning you: It's a trap and you will regret it!

Don't waste years of your life trying to recover from something you could totally avoid.

Look beyond the bait and see the hook. Satan wants to get his hooks so deep into your personal affairs that you literally die inside. That's exactly what could happen if you give in or continue to give in to this fleshly desire/temptation/lure.

Don't allow a person to be what only God can be in your life. God wants to fill this emptiness inside you. God wants to comfort you, strengthen you, help you. That's why He sent the Holy Spirit. (John 14:26)

How Well Do You Know Yourself?

My husband says I'm very predictable. No matter what restaurant we eat at, he can order off the menu for me without even asking. I rarely ever venture out of my "comfort zone" and typically order the same few menu items over and over.

Well, Satan thinks you're pretty predictable too. He knows you. He knows your weaknesses. He knows where you are most easily tempted to forfeit God's plan for the "next best thing," the counterfeit plan.

If your weakness is premarital sex, he knows that. That's exactly why he keeps bringing that specific temptation into your life over and over. He knows just how far you'll go. He knows exactly how to grab your attention. If you're single and you have demonstrated that sex before marriage is a major temptation for you, then you can count on it, you will be faced with much opportunity to give in to this weakness.

Satan is constantly looking for ways to set you up. He will arrange for you to be alone with someone of the opposite sex. He will strategically bring people back into your life with whom you've been intimate in the past. He will subtly convince you to sleep with them again because, "Hey, what does it matter? You've already been together. What's it gonna hurt?" It's a trap!

This "lure" may seem attractive now but when you wake up from this "hook up" it's not going to seem so enticing. Who would have thought that one kiss with the wrong person would lead to divorce from a twenty year marriage, isolation from your teenage kids, losing your job, your home, your friends, your confidence, and your peace of mind. Satan wants you to feel dirty, de-valued, ashamed, rejected, guilty and used. It's a trap. Refocus your attention. Get your eyes off the bait and stay alert to the hook behind it.

Think back over your life. Where have you had the most struggles? Be honest with yourself. I want you to seriously *think of the outcome* before you give in.

What are you going to say to your parents?

How will you address this affair with your children?

What about your co-workers?

Imagine your situation being on the front page of the newspaper tomorrow morning. Are you ashamed? Do you want to hide from your neighbors?

Satan doesn't want you thinking reality thoughts. He wants you to remain in "la-la land" just thinking about how amazing he/she makes you feel.

Feelings lie

You might argue at this point, "No, they don't, Terri. I have never felt this way about someone. He just happens to be married." Remember this, God would never arrange for two people to get together under those circumstances. That's not how God works. And if God's hand isn't in it, then you should't want any part of it.

I know that's blunt and to the point, but you need someone pointing out the truth to you. Why? Because the truth will set you free. Remember, tomorrow morning always comes. Wake up with no regrets.

Psalm 51:6 says, "Behold, You desire truth in the inward parts, and in the hidden part You will make me to know wisdom" (*NKJV*).

I want you to be painstakingly honest with yourself about yourself. How are you going to feel tomorrow morning when you wake up after giving in to a temptation last night? How will you feel when he/she never calls you again? How will you feel when you've been promising God you're not going to do this anymore? How will you feel when you're staring at your phone and it just won't ring? How will you feel when you look at his/her Facebook status and it still says, "Single" or "Married". What does that do to your heart? That's the reality. I want you to realize the Bible says "When you are tempted" (James 1:13) and not "if you are tempted".

You will be tempted. I will be tempted. But it's what we do when temptation comes that matters. Don't repeat this year what you did last year. Time is ticking. Your calling is calling. And Satan is vying for your attention. He is pulling out all the stops using whatever bait he can to lure you away from God and His plan for your life. If he can get you to glance in his direction, desire what he is offering, he knows it's just a matter of time and you're hooked.

Romans 13 says, "We can't afford to waste a minute, must not squander these precious daylight hours in frivolity and indulgence, in sleeping around and dissipation, in bickering and grabbing everything in sight. Get out of bed and get dressed! Don't loiter and linger, waiting until the very last minute. Dress yourselves in Christ and be up and about" (*THE MESSAGE*)!

Your life is too precious and too valuable to God for you to waste it on a wrong relationship. The time to get serious is now. God has so much for you to do. I'm going to give you practical tips to guide you through this breaking up process. You will never regret moving on.

"I just ended a relationship that I felt God telling me to sever for a very long time. I tried so many times to maintain the relationship and justify the wrong that we were doing. We had a history with one another. So you can imagine the thoughts that were helping to continue to justify why I should stay in the relationship. It's been a few days since I left, but I had to leave quickly and obey God before this unholy soul tie continued. Thanks for the information because it is empowering me to obey God, stay away from my past relationship, and continue in faith."

- AJ

Chapter 5

The Greener the Grass, the Greater the Deception

I have a dear friend who was getting ready for church one early Sunday morning at her apartment in Fort Worth, Texas. A single girl, graduate from Oral Roberts University, beautiful inside and out and still a virgin at 22 years old. On this ordinary Autumn morning, she was attacked.

Dressed in her bathrobe and applying her make-up, she heard a knock at the door. As she went to see who would be visiting this early on a weekend morning, she asked, "Who is it?" On the other side of that door she heard, "It's maintenance. I'm here to check your air conditioning unit." Not realizing there was anything wrong with her unit, she asked suspiciously, "Why are you checking my unit? Is there something wrong with it?" Acknowledging her by name and sounding very convincing, he said, "Yes, Janet. The apartment manager, Vicki, sent me this morning."

"Hmmmm…he knows my name. He knows the manager's name. I guess it's safe," she thought as she cracked open the door. And that's all it took.

That one little crack of the door led to the fight of her life.

This "apartment employee" came barging in. He pushed the door open and began attacking her. Chasing her into her bedroom and wrestling to get her robe off of her and ultimately violate her, the struggle was on. Janet began yelling the name of Jesus over and over at him. Each time, he would calm down. Then, he would began to attack again.

Calling on the power that's in the name of Jesus was her best and her only defense against

> That one little crack of the door led to the fight of her life.

him. Supernaturally, God saved her from this attacker as she was able to divert his attention and run out the front door unharmed. The moral of that story is *don't open the door*.

Your mind is the door-keeper for what you will eventually do.

The evil one is constantly knocking on the door of your heart looking for any entrance into your life. Once you open the door to him through your unguarded thought life, the fight is on. You are in a war and it's a war for your life. It's not a war that you can see with your eyes or fight with your hands—it's a spiritual battle. Your flesh and your spirit are continually at war with each other (see Gal. 5:17).

If the door is already open in your life and you feel that you are fighting to break free from this soul tie, you need the Word of God to build you up like never before. You cannot fight this battle alone. You need God on your side.

Sometimes we do things that seem so minor or insignificant but they lead to major setbacks in our lives.

Who would have thought:

A simple Facebook comment could lead to a full on adulterous affair?

A single marijuana joint could lead to 14 years behind bars?

One casual drink could lead to being a college drop-out attending Alcoholics Anonymous classes?

One cheap bet on a college football game could lead to a gambling addiction?

One single mouse-click could lead to a porn addiction?

One swipe of the credit card could lead to bankruptcy and financial bondage?

That's how Satan works. Little by little we are attracting in our lives the very things we do not want. Destruction. Ruin. Failure. Disappointments. Regret. Daily, we are given the choice to do the right things or give in to the wrong things. We are the ones who choose to actively open the door or keep it closed.

Satan knows you're not going to *knowingly* fall into sin. So he has to deceive you into thinking it's something good. It's something you need. It's not anything that will harm you. He is a liar and the father of all lies. He is incapable of telling the truth. If your life is veering off the path of God, then that reveals who you are spending more time listening to. A liar.

It's not a coincidence

I received an email from a friend warning women about the common traits of rapists. It was very informative about their similar strategies.

Timing: Rapists usually attack between the hours of 5:00 and 8:30 A.M.

Appearance: Rapists tend to target women with long hair. The first thing they look for in a victim is hairstyle. A woman wearing a pony tail, bun or braid is the easiest to be grabbed.

Places: The number one place where women are abducted is in grocery store parking lots.

Distracted: The attackers look for women on their cell phone, searching through their purse or doing other activities while walking because they are caught off-guard and can be easily overpowered.

When I read this email, my first thought was how Satan works the same way in his efforts to destroy our lives through wrong soul ties.

His timing is very well thought-out. He seems to attack us or bring distractions in our lives when we are weak, fatigued, stressed or haven't spent as much quality time with God. He also works especially hard right before God is getting ready to promote us. The timing is very strategic.

Where Satan attacks us, *who* he uses and *how* he does it are all part of his plan. Trust me, there is method to his madness. Nothing about your soul tie to this person is coincidental. He hopes to wipe both of you out.

Remember this, Satan doesn't bother too many people who aren't doing much for God. When he feels a threat coming on, he pulls out all the stops. He must see something in you that perhaps you're not seeing in yourself. I know, personally, my biggest and most intense battles have come right before God was getting ready to promote me and do a new thing in my life. I always think back to how hopeless I felt during the battle and "if I had only known what was coming". I thank God that I learned to fight Satan and so I can enjoy what God is doing in my life today.

Have you been deceived into something good?

When I was in college, I began to let down my guard and gradually, I accepted things that I never thought I would do or permit. I was like that frog experiment in Biology class. He jumped out of the boiling hot water as if to say, "Are you kidding me? I'm not an idiot! Get me out of here!" The same frog was placed in a pot of cool water and the heat was gradually turned up little by little. He just sat there comfortably until he cooked to death! Like the frog, slowly I began to conform to my environment and without even realizing it, I was choosing death over life.

What is deception? It's believing a lie and not realizing you've done so. Well, if you believe a lie, then to you it's the truth!

Hebrews 3:12 says, "Watch out! Don't let evil thoughts or doubts make any of you turn from the living God" (*CEV*). Satan works through deception. Mac Hammond says, "Deception isn't just one of the ways the devil can bring the effects of the curse into your life—it is the only way."

Satan is not going to show up at your front door with a red costume and a pitch fork on Friday the 13th and say, "I'm here to deceive you. Come with me." Nobody would fall for that. He has to disguise himself.

"For Satan himself transforms himself into an angel of light" (2 Cor. 11:14, *NKJV*).

Make note: He smells good. He looks good. He sounds good. He tastes good. He feels good. He makes you feel good. He relaxes you. He appeals to your senses. He flatters you. He adores you. He compliments you. He relieves your stress. He makes you look good. He is fun (for a season). He plays on your emotions and satisfies your desires. He makes sin look good. Very good.

Going back to the original sin of Adam and Eve, how did Satan convince Eve to give in to the temptation to eat the forbidden fruit? Out of all the trees in the garden that she had access to, how was he able to convince her that she couldn't live without the one tree in the whole garden that God said she could not have? He deceived her into thinking she was missing out.

Satan simply presents that 20% that you don't have in life and whispers, "This is what you're missing. This is all you need to feel complete. How can you go your whole life without this 20%? Life would be perfect if you had this 20%. This is the one thing missing in your life."

The Word of God declares that the lust of the flesh and the lust of the eyes are not of God but of the world (see 1 John 2:16). Whatever Satan is bringing before your eyes seducing you into thinking you cannot live without it, it's only 20%. Don't lose the 80% you have. Stay focused.

Today, you will most likely not encounter a talking snake, but Satan will slither his way into your life with some forbidden and very appealing thing that tempts you. It could be another person, a substance, a career, a sexual temptation, a pornographic website. It's 20%.

Jesse Duplantis says, "The greener the grass, the greater the deception."

"Be well balanced (temperate, sober of mind), be vigilant and cautious at all times; for that enemy of yours, the devil, roams around like a lion roaring (in fierce hunger), seeking someone to seize upon and devour" (1 Pet. 5:8, AMP).

I love the next verse too, "Withstand him; be firm in faith (against his onset—rooted, established, strong, immovable, and determined), knowing that the same (identical) sufferings are appointed to your brotherhood (the whole body of Christians) throughout the world" (Pet. 5:9, *AMP*).

In other words: You are not alone. Your temptations (no matter how secret they may be) are not uncommon. We all face temptations.

Keep in mind, his roar is designed to paralyze you with fear.

The devil can't devour just anyone. His roar is designed to help him identify whom he may devour. Why does he come at you as a roaring lion? The same reason a real lion roars at its prey: to paralyze them with fear. If you yield to that fear he will devour you.

"Sin is crouching at the door, eager to control you. But you must subdue it and be its master" (Gen. 4:7, *NLT*).

Satan has a keen way of making us justify sin. As I mentioned earlier, it's not overnight. Little by little, we compromise. Justifying sin is saying, "Is it really wrong? Doesn't God want me to be happy? I'm not the only one who's done this. God will forgive me."

I want you to recognize where a door may have been opened in your life or in your thought life and determine to close it. Don't fall for Satan's disguises and tricks. Pay attention to what you're giving your attention to. You will stay miserable if you do not get your attention back on God and His Word.

If you choose to stay in a relationship that you know deep in your heart is not God's will for your life, you are choosing death.

So what do you do when you've opened the door to something wrong?

1. Confess the sin.

Satan still has you trapped wherever there is unconfessed sin in your life. And the fact that you keep returning to the same sin is no excuse for not confessing. Get sin out of your life. Get alone with God and ask Him to forgive you.

> *"If we confess our sins, he is faithful and just to forgive us our sins and cleanse us from all unrighteousness"* (1 John 1:9, NKJV).

God forgives you the first time you ask. Don't let Satan, the Accuser, keep harassing you with guilt and shame over your past. That's another trap. Receive forgiveness once and for all.

> *"For I will forgive their wickedness and will remember their sins no more"* (Heb. 8:12, *NIV*).

2. Renounce the sin.

This is something I learned from Stormie Omartian. She said, "You can't be delivered from something you have not *completely* put out of your life."

Stormie explains, "Confessing is speaking the whole truth about your sin. Renouncing is taking a firm stand against it and removing its right to stay."

Did you read that? You must remove its right to stay in your life. What does that mean? Get it out of your sight, out of your home, out of your car, out of your office, off your computer, off your phone, and out of your thought life.

You will never regret doing this. As intense as the pain will be when you first say "No more," there will come a day when you praise God enthusiastically because you're free. Your mind will not be tormented.

Your spirit will not be heavy. Your soul will not be in knots. You will be free.

Later, I am going to take you on a walk through your house and we will launch a thorough house cleaning to rid you of any things that are keeping you attached to this person. You will experience another level of healing and freedom by doing this. We are talking about your future, your destiny, your calling. Don't let Satan in any part of your life. You can do this.

3. Forgive yourself.

I've had a harder time with this than with forgiving those who have hurt me. It's not easy when you have let yourself down over and over. You must choose by faith to forgive yourself and accept that you are human and you make mistakes.

You serve a loving God who never consults your past to determine your future. This is vital. Shame and guilt will keep you from your calling. Say it, "I choose to forgive myself by faith in Jesus' Name." You may need to say this daily, as I have, in order for it to really sink in. This is a big step to your freedom.

4. Receive God's love for you.

You must accept that God loves you. His love covers a multitude of sins (1 Peter 4:8). He loves you just as much today as He did two years ago, last month, and last night. There's nothing you can do to make Him love you more or less. And it's *your choice* to receive it or reject it.

Jeremiah 31:3-4 says, "I have loved you with an everlasting love; Therefore I have drawn you with lovingkindness. Again I will build you and you will be rebuilt" (*NAS*).

God wants to rebuild your life. Satan wants you to think that you've messed up too bad, given in to too many temptations for God to truly love you or ever use you. He knows that receiving God's love will change everything in your life.

Hebrews 4:15 says, "For we do not have a High Priest who cannot sympathize with our weaknesses, but was in all points tempted as we are, yet without sin" (*NAS*).

Jesus was tempted. He understands. And that's why He intercedes on our behalf before God. He loves you. God's love casts out fear (the fear of never being able to recover from what you've been through, the fear of falling again, the fear of never being able to be used of God after what you've done, the fear of others, etc.).

Receiving His love for you personally will cast that fear right out of your life. His love is what has given me the confidence and courage to do what I'm doing today. God's love never fails (see 1 Cor. 13:8). *Never means never.*

God wants to do something in your life. He wants to do *a new thing.* But the old things must be removed so he can bring in the new.

"As of last year, I had been a virgin for 20 years and I was hoping to keep myself until I got married. Unfortunately I didn't, and it was actually the woman I believe God had brought into my life which made it worse.

For more than 3 months of guilt, shame, and condemnation over what I had done, and being scared to come to God, being stuck in a sinful cycle and giving up the thought of God ever using me or truly loving me, I want to thank God for letting you write your book, <u>Make Your Dreams Bigger Than Your Memories</u>.

My life has completed changed, I am ready to let go of my past, all the things that weigh me down and step into the dreams and vision for my life. I thank God for your life once again."

- Richard

Chapter 6

As Close As
You Want To Be

Two months after I got my driver's license at age 16, I was at home one rainy Monday night doing my homework. I ran out of paper so I jumped in my brand new red Ford Mustang convertible and headed for the store. When I got to the stop sign at the end of our street, I put on my brakes but the car slid in a 180 degree turn on the wet pavement. As I was sliding, a car going 50 miles per hour hit me head on.

Everything went black. I don't remember anything except lights coming at me and then waking up later seated in the passenger's side of my car. I thought I was dreaming. I could not comprehend what was happening. I got out of the car and just stared at my car in the ditch trying to understand. I felt something pouring down my face and when I reached up to feel my head it was gashed wide open. My head had actually cracked the front windshield.

I kept putting my fingers in the open wound on my head trying to understand what was going on. The blood was pouring out all over me. Then, I began running down the street yelling, "My head is dented in! My head is dented in!" A man who stopped because of the accident put a towel over my head and held it until the ambulance arrived.

Next thing I knew, I was sitting in an ambulance and the paramedic was wiping the blood off my face. I couldn't help but think about him taking my make up off and how I really wished he wouldn't. That's when they knew I was totally conscious!

He asked, "Are you hurting anywhere?"

I said, "Yes. It's hurts so bad!" I pulled up my jogging pants on my right leg to show him where the pain was excruciating and there it was: *a tiny, little scratch across my knee.* He simply wiped the blood off. Meanwhile, my head was gashed wide open with arteries hanging out, but all I could feel was the little scratch on my knee.

What I've realized is that when we're hurt in life, *we tend to focus on minor things when the real issue is left untouched.* To finish the story, I had to get stitches on the inside and outside of my head, and then they allowed my mom to take me home. I realized through this painful experience that as I began to recover, *the healing process can be more painful than the initial injury.* As the days went by, my stomach muscles became so sore that it became more and more difficult to get in and out of bed. The bruises on my face began to turn dark purple, and my right eye turned bloodshot after about three days.

When word got out about my wreck, all my friends wanted to come by and check on me. As each one visited, they all wanted to see the wound and talk about it. And each time I pulled the bandages back and exposed the wound, I delayed the healing process. Did you read that? I wasn't letting it completely heal as long as I kept exposing it. Not only that, but the more I talked about it, the more I increased my fear of driving again.

Healing from the inside out

I've discovered how this accident parallels what we face when we encounter situations that hurt and wound us in life. Many times we deal with the effects of our hurts and not the cause of the hurts. But God wants to deal with the root issue. Not only that, but the truth is that the healing process hurts, and it may take longer than we thought in order to be totally made whole.

As long as we keep talking about our pasts, exposing our wounds to every new set of ears, we are delaying our own recovery. God wants to heal you everywhere you hurt, but He also wants to deal with the root issue. He said in Jeremiah 30:17, "For I will restore health to you and heal you of your wounds,' says the Lord" (*NKJV*).

Satan works from the day you are born to bring hurts into your life. He is no respecter of persons. He wants you wounded, bruised and broken on the inside so you'll never be whole and confident to walk out your purpose. We've all been hurt at different times in our lives, some more severely than others. Some hurts are only on the surface and not too bad, others go deep and leave a *permanent scar* in our minds and affect us for years, maybe even a lifetime.

Perhaps you were severely wounded emotionally. Maybe you experienced a great deal of rejection, betrayal, or abuse. Although you've blocked it out and moved on, you still don't feel that you're doing all that God wants you to do. Perhaps something still isn't totally right in you and it's keeping you back.

I know I hid all of my pain behind one big band-aid. I just covered it up. Band-aids don't heal us on their own. They don't medicate or heal deep wounds. They hide the wound and make everything look fine. And that's what I did. I went through some very painful experiences of rejection and *I hid every bit of it* behind a giant band-aid of activities, a big smile, and accomplishments. Meanwhile, I was hurt and bleeding on the inside.

When you're bleeding inside it's eventually going to show up on the outside in your behavior, your attitude, your moods, your relationships, your career, your self-image, your overall choices. Since I felt so bad about myself inside, I had to do things on the outside to feel better. I didn't know that was why I was doing it. You may be thinking, "I'm fine. What I went through was so long ago. I'm over it." I thought I was too, until God began to show me little by little where I needed

> God will change your circumstances, but He'll change you first.

some major healing.

Let me ask you this:

Do you find at times you have no real passion for anything?

Do the smallest things wear you out at times?

Do you lack vision, purpose and meaning to your life?

Do you wonder why you're even here?

Do you feel like you're in a rut? Just existing?

Do you get excited about pursuing God and His plan for your life only to find that four days later that passion is gone?

Do you start things, get bored, and never finish them?

Things will never be right *around* you until they are first right *in* you. God will change your circumstances, but He'll change *you* first. Just because we ignore something doesn't make it go away.

What happened in your situation with a wrong soul tie? How has it affected your personality? Who hurt you? Who rejected you? Who belittled you? Who violated you? Who made you feel that you weren't as good as someone else? Is there a name? Or a face that comes to mind? Did you use to be fun or funny and now you just go through the motions of life? What memories are you still re-playing in your mind? Did you use to have dreams and goals?

Are you going to sit back and allow an experience or a person stop you from doing what God put you on this earth to do? You may be crying out for God's next step in your life, "God, what do you want me to do with my life?" He's saying, "Get healed."

When our military troops are wounded in the war, they pull them off the front lines and let them heal. They're no good out there fighting while hurt and beat up you're trying to fight the devil with one eye shut, one arm in a sling and on crutches, you are not going to win in that condition. You've got to get healed.

Isaiah 61:1 says, "He has sent me to bind up the brokenhearted" (*NIV*). *The Message* version says, "To heal the heartbroken…and comfort all who mourn." Luke 4:18 (*The Message*) says that Jesus came to "release the oppressed" and "set the burdened and battered free." Jesus came to set the captives free; Satan came to take the free captive.

Satan wants to keep you trapped in something from your past—what you've done or what's been done to you. Obviously, God knew Satan was out to break our hearts and steal our dreams or He wouldn't have sent Jesus to be the Healer of the Brokenhearted.

Make a Diagnosis

As I began seeking God for my own healing, I discovered that in order to be healed, you first have to diagnose the problem. You could be taking all the wrong medicines if you don't know where you're sick. Last year, I was experiencing so much pain when I would chew my food and then try to swallow it. People thought it was the flu, strep throat, sinus infection, stress, ulcer, etc. They were recommending all different types of medicine. Finally, I went to the doctor myself, and she ran the tests. Once diagnosed, they could prescribe the right medicine. If I had never allowed someone to diagnose the problem I could have wasted time and money trying everything to get better.

You could be thinking that a new husband is going to fix the loneliness you feel in your current marriage. Or that a little cosmetic surgery will give you the confidence you've lacked your whole life. Or that a promotion will heal your insecurities. Or that having a baby will bring joy back into your life. Nothing on the outside is going to change the way you feel on the inside.

It wasn't until I began seeking God that I discovered my true problem. I used to think that I was just shy. That was my excuse for not going to certain parties or being around certain people. Or I would think, "I'm just humble. I don't have to be around the 'big wigs' to feel important." So I would avoid certain social events, avoid going in the "speakers rooms" with the famous preachers. It wasn't humility. It wasn't shyness. It was a fear of rejection. As God began to reveal this to me, He showed me different times in my life where I was severely rejected and treated as having no value or second best. I carried that into other relationships and experienced more rejection with more wrong soul ties. What you think about, you attract.

I had the diagnosis for my problem. I had a major fear of rejection. I truly thought deep down inside that I wasn't good enough, that I was ugly and I would be rejected. Now that I knew the problem, I could treat it.

How do you discover the root problem in your life? As with any illness, you have to seek out the physician. In our case, that's God. He is the Great Physician. This is something only you can do for yourself. Nobody can go to the Physician for you. Have you ever been so sick that you don't even want to get out of bed, but you know you need to go to the doctor? You can't send your friend. You can't send your Pastor. You can't send your spouse or your mom. *You have to do this for yourself.*

As I began studying this message, I thought about when you visit a doctor's office. They don't run a check-up on you in the waiting room in front of everyone. They don't run your tests in the lobby. It's in private. The doctor meets with you in a room alone, then visits you *privately* to run your tests. What am I saying? Get alone with God. He is the Great Physician. Healing always take place on the inside before it ever shows up on the outside.

If you're one of those types like I was who avoids solitude and quietness, then you're going to have to get comfortable being alone with no noise in the background. Shut the door, turn the cell phone off, turn the music off, turn the TV off, turn Facebook off, and get alone with God. Talk to Him. Tell Him everything. Don't hold anything back.

When you're alone with Him, receive His love. *God's love is the cure* for every wound in your life. His love is unconditional.

When you had that abortion, He still loved you.

When you got in that wrong relationship, He still loved you.

When you got out of church for a while, He still loved you.

When you made promises you couldn't keep, He still loved you.

When you stopped talking with him, He still loved you.

When you were hurt, rejected, and abused, He still loved you.

Isaiah 49:16 says that God even has you tattooed on the palm of His hand. In other words, parents weren't the first ones to carry around little "brag books" of their children. God started that. He just whips out His photos of you right there on the palm of His hand.

> God's love is the cure for every wound in your life.

How do you receive that healing when you're alone with Him? Worshiping God for "Who you need Him to be" brings healing. If your foot is hurting, you don't go to the heart specialist. You go to a podiatrist. If your heart isn't beating right, you don't go to the eye doctor. You go to a cardiologist. Well, if your heart is broken and wounded inside, you don't need to seek God as your Financial Provider. You seek God, the Healer, Jehovah Rapha, the Healer of the Brokenhearted.

There's a story in Matthew 8 of a leper who is in need of healing. Verse 2 says, "'Look! A leper is approaching,' He *kneels before him (Jesus) worshiping.* 'Sir, the leper pleads, 'if you want to, you can heal me.' Jesus touches the man. 'I want to,' he says, 'Be healed.' And *instantly* the leprosy disappears" (The Living Bible).

Notice 3 things from this story about the leper:

1. He wasn't asking the Lord for a financial miracle. He sought the Lord as his healer. He actually *cried out* to Him. God hears your cries every time you call out to Him.

2. He bowed down and worshipped Jesus *before* he got his healing. When we bow down and surrender all of our hurts to God *while we're still hurting*, we are showing our faith in God.

3. Jesus said, "I want to." In other words, it is God's will that you be healed from everything that hurts you. It's one thing to doubt God's ability, it's another thing to doubt His willingness.

God not only wants to heal your heart and restore your soul, but He wants you made whole. What does being made whole mean? You can get to a place in your life where there are *no signs* you were ever sick before. No signs of emotional abuse. No signs of sexual abuse. No signs of physical abuse. No signs of dysfunction. No signs of depression. No signs of rejection. No signs you were ever hurt before. That's wholeness.

How do you get there? Quiet time with God. There is nothing in your life more important than spending quality, consistent time with God. Everything you could ever need is found in His presence. Joy, confidence, peace, direction, security, hope, comfort, rest—everything is found in the presence of God.

"He who dwells in the secret place of the most high shall remain stable..." (Psalm 91:1, *AMP*)

Are you up one day and down the next? Do you wonder "What is wrong with me?" Are you tormented with thoughts of your past and that person day and night? Are you excited about life one day and then, overnight it seems like you just wake up depressed, discouraged and feeling hopeless? Time with God is the answer to bringing stability in your emotions.

How do you get started spending focused time with God?

1. Schedule God on your calendar.

As John Maxwell says, "Priorities never stay put." We have to make ourselves schedule our priorities on our daily schedules or something will always interrupt our plans. If there's anything Satan does not want you to do, it's spending quality time with God. Why? He knows everything will change and he will lose his hold on you.

2. Set the atmosphere. Plan ahead.

Don't plan to spend your quiet time with God in a room that's cluttered and messy. Why? Because you will be distracted and want to start cleaning it. I speak from experience. Remember Satan looks for *anything* to distract you from communicating with God. If it's a messy room, he'll see to it that you start organizing. Before you know it, your time is gone.

Take a CD or MP3 player in your room. Get it out the night before so you don't waste time in the morning trying to search for it and use up all the time you wanted to spend with God. You can tell that I've been down this road a few times.

Find or purchase some worship music. I did that years ago and now, when I play that one certain worship album, it just makes me cry. I truly believe that it welcomes the presence of the Holy Spirit.

3. Change it up.

If every time I saw my best friend, we went to the same place, talked about the same things and spent the same amount of time together, it would get old. We would both get bored with each other.

You don't have to pray the same prayers over and over and over.

Here are some other ideas for spending focused time with God:

- **Take photos** of people to pray over.

- **Read a verse** from one of the Psalms.

> If there's anything Satan does not want you to do, it's spending quality time with God.

- **Read a Proverb** for the day (there are 31 Proverbs; one for each day of the month).

- Read a daily devotional.

- Take a list of Scriptures to confess (to speak out of your mouth). That's one of the most powerful things you can do to see change in your life.

- Make a list of things you're thankful for and verbalize your gratitude toward God. Even if you feel as if you have nothing to be thankful for at this moment in your life, you do. Stop looking at what's lost in your life and look around at what's left. Begin thanking the Lord for what you have left and watch Him move in your life.

You can say, "Lord, I just want you to know how thankful I am for…this house, my health, my job, my children, my salary, the food we have, the vacation we took, etc."

Psalm 100:4 says, "Be thankful and say so" (*AMP*). It opens the door for God to begin blessing your life!

- Take a list of positive confessions to pray over yourself. You need to hear yourself speaking positive affirmations and declarations.

"I'm confident."

"I'm secure."

"I'm highly favored of God."

"I'm blessed and very successful."

"I'm beautiful inside and out."

"I'm fun to be around."

"I'm proactive."

"I'm in the best shape of my life."

- Sing. There's a certain release that happens inside of us when we sing songs out of our spirit to God. He loves it. Other people may not, but God finds it heavenly. Sing worship songs you've heard at church or just make up words to your loving Heavenly Father.

- Journal your time with God. I do this every time I spend quiet time with the Lord. I always take a journal and a pen with me. I just sit quietly and listen. God wants to speak to you. He may just speak one word quietly to your spirit. Write down everything you hear, even if you're not sure if it's God or just you. Write it down anyway. Get into a habit of hearing from God.

Let me give you a hint: don't be in such a hurry to hear from God that if you don't hear something within 45 seconds, you just assume He doesn't speak to you. Sit quietly. You need that stillness and quietness in your life. Just listen. Whatever you feel in your spirit, write it down. Even though your mind may be convincing you that it isn't God speaking, write it down anyway. I can't tell you how many times I've done this and the whole time I was thinking, "That's not God; that's Terri." Later, I would go back and read what I wrote down and think, "Wait! That had to be God!"

4. Be consistent.

Time with God is no different than working out or dieting. You have to give it attention first, then you begin to desire it, then changes begin to show up.

If you work out for seven days and see no changes, it's not that the treadmill doesn't work. You just haven't done it long enough to see changes. You have to keep at it. God wants to do so much more in your life, but He has to have time with you.

"If you want to see change in your life, change something you do daily."
- John Maxwell

You can spend daily time with God even while you're driving to work or school or cooking dinner or folding laundry or sitting at your desk. Be aware that He's always there. He is ever present just waiting to hear from you. He's such a gentleman, He waits for you to make the first move (James 4:7-8).

If you can do something consistently for 21 days, you can break an old habit and start a new one. Set a goal to spend the next 21 days with God and start with five minutes a day. You can do that. You can start this habit that will change the course of your life.

When you spend consistent time with God, He will:

· Heal your heart
· Restore your soul (mind, will, emotions)
· Give you the direction you've longed for
· Help you make those hard decisions
· Give you the strength to get out of sin
· Give you peace if your mind is tormented
· Give you courage to step away from a controlling person
· Reveal His plan for your life
· Love on you and make you feel secure.

You can get as close as you want to be. It's up to you. God is just standing there with open arms ready to be what only He can be in your life—your everything.

"Seeing my ex is torture."

"I am so glad that I found your ministry. I read your email today about the guilt and shame that you felt. And now I read about "Intimate Soul Ties". You described my situation perfectly. Now I understand why I am having such a difficult time letting go.

All I do is pray and cry and it doesn't help that I see my ex almost everyday since we live a block away from each other. Seeing my ex with someone else daily is torture for me. It's been since January 2009 since the demise of our relationship after 15 years. I moved back to my home state to take care of my elderly parents for the last 10 yrs. My Mom had a stroke 15 yrs ago and is completely paralyzed on the right side. Right now I am overwhelmed in my life and I ask God daily to heal me and to give me the strength to keep going. I have been seeing a therapist and I am on depression meds but nothing seems to be helping me. If it weren't for the fact that my mom needs me so much, I would just give up. I will get your book in the hope that it will assist me in the healing process."

- Janis

Chapter 7

The One Thing You Need
When It's Over

Have you been to the Eiffel Tower?

Have you been on a cruise?

Have you read <u>Rich Dad, Poor Dad</u>?

Have you taken a train anywhere?

Have you studied a foreign language?

Have you ever written a check for $1,000 to a charitable work?

Have you ever run a marathon?

Have you been to Disney World?

Have you sung in public?

Have you written a book?

Have you read the Bible from start to finish?

God has so much for you to do with the life you have left. Proverbs 29:18 says it plainly, "Where there is no vision, the people perish" (*KJV*). I looked up the word *perish*, and it means *die*. I looked up the word *die*, and it means *die!* I say that to be funny but it is imperative that you have a vision to get up tomorrow morning. I want you to understand that if you are not looking towards something, you will automatically go back to what's familiar.

A person with no vision will always return to their past.

I have seen other people's advice on how to get over a breakup include recommendations such as: cry as hard as you can, assess what went wrong in the relationship, listen to break-up music, go outside, and feel the pain. At this point, you've probably done those *tremendous* tips a thousand times and where has it gotten you? In the same place you were last week at this time.

The one thing you need more than anything else is vision. You need a goal to aim towards. It could be anything from:

· Getting closer to God than ever before
· Being at your perfect weight
· Being debt-free
· Going on a dream trip with your closest friends
· Having a new job
· Cleaning out your house and get organized
· Moving to a new location

The battleground is in your mind. If you want to sit around and relive every moment you had together, all the intimate words shared and the promises that you thought would last forever, you will stay miserable. If you want to move on and enjoy the life God has given you, then you must get a vision, a dream, a goal to focus towards.

"Loneliness is not the absence of affection; but the absence of direction."
– Mike Murdoch

I have given you some direction in the areas of drawing closer to God and spending consistent time with Him. But in the last few chapters, I will challenge you to set new goals for your finances, your body, and your organization at home that will revitalize your spirit and I believe will catapult you out of the past and into an exciting new future.

> The one thing you need more than anything else is vision. You need a goal to aim towards.

Warning: there are factors that could stop you from moving beyond where you're at today. So before you even allow these "dream thieves" to enter your thought life, I'm going to warn you of them right now.

I want you to recognize the following as "dream thieves":

1. Time

If you're like most people coming out of a painful relationship situation, you could look back and say, "Wow, I really wasted my time with him!" How long were you together? Was it a short-lived romance? Or did it go on for many months or even years making it even harder to shake off and move ahead?

Perhaps you're looking back and you feel the time is now wasted. I want you to know that you have not wasted time. No matter how good or bad the relationship was, you did not waste time. God has a way of using every experience in our lives to shape us into what He created us to be.

As painful as some of my soul ties have been, I realize that I would not be who I am today had I not gone through those painful times. When the emails come in with questions on soul ties, I get it. I know the pain. I know how long it can take to recover. I know when someone says, "Just get over it," they haven't been there. They don't know that it's just not possible to nonchalantly "get over". It takes time and a plan.

On the other hand, how much time has passed since you last dreamed? Does it look like your dreams and goals will never happen so you might as well give up on them? Do you feel so behind already?

Have you lost sight of your dreams because of how much *time* has passed?

Have you ever heard someone say, "I always wanted to be a teacher, but I got married young and that just never happened." Ten years later, they are still saying the same thing. They could have been a teacher by then!

Think about how long Joseph sat in a dark prison hoping one day his dream would really come to pass. Thirteen painful, agonizing, dark and dim years went by and I'm sure he felt hopeless, but he didn't give up on his dreams. He did not allow time to be a distraction to what he saw in his spirit. God accelerated his dreams. And He can accelerate yours. Don't let time stop you from dreaming.

Genesis 41:14, 41: So Pharaoh sent for Joseph, and he was quickly brought from the dungeon...So Pharaoh said to Joseph, "I hereby put you in charge of the whole land of Egypt" (*NIV*).

God still has plenty of time to use you. Remember, there is no neutral with God. We are either going forward or we are going backward. Don't let time just go by being inactive, passive, and doing nothing. You don't have another year to waste. It's time to do something with the time you have left.

2. Age

How old are you now? How young are you? Are you concerned that you're getting older and wonder who is going to want to marry you? Have you lived more of your life than you have left? Is your mind telling you that you've missed your golden opportunities to fulfill your dreams? "You're getting old." "It's too late now." "Just forget it!" Are you wishing you had started a long time ago? Are you comparing yourself to other people and looking at what all they have accomplished? Perhaps they are even quite a bit younger than you?

Stop looking at the years you have lost and look at the years you have left. Do something with the years you have ahead of you.

Abraham was 99 years old when he finally saw his dream come to pass of having a son. He didn't give up. Why should you?

Colonel Sanders of Kentucky Fried Chicken was 66 years old when he decided he did not want to live off of his Social Security checks so he started a fastfood restaurant.

Joyce Meyer was 42 years old when she launched out into her

own full-time ministry.

CoCo Chanel was 71 when she debuted the Chanel suit.

Ronald Reagan was 73 when he was re-elected as President of the United States of America.

Brooke Sheilds was 11 months when she was hired for her first television commerical as the Ivory Snow baby.

Shirley Temple began her film career at 4, and three years later received an Academy Award.

You are not too young and you are not too old to accomplish those dreams in your heart. Satan will lie to anyone who will listen. You have to actively stop listening to his lies and get filled up with God's truth.

3. Words.

Are you allowing someone else's lousy opinion of you to determine whether or not you are going to do what God called you to do? Remember this: when you stand before God on Judgment Day, you will stand responsible for *your* life not *their* life.

Words can have such power over us—if we let them.

"You're a loser."
"You're damaged goods."
"That dream is ridiculous."
"Who do you think you are."
"You always mess things up."
"Give it up. It's never going to happen."

Many people have heard the success story of basketball Hall of Famer Michael Jordan being cut from the sophomore basketball team. But what if he had allowed the words "you didn't make the team" to stop him from pursuing his dream? What if? Words did not stop him from dreaming. Why should they stop you?

Albert Einstein and Edgar Allen Poe were expelled from school for being mentally slow. What does that tell you?

I read that at one time, Oprah Winfrey was an evening news reporter; however, the producers thought she was too emotionally invested in her stories. Eventually, Baltimore's WJZ-TV pulled her off the air. As a consolation, they offered her a role on a daytime TV show. At that time, taking a daytime TV spot was considered a huge step down from the evening news spot she once held. After relocating to Chicago, she hosted a fledgling morning news show and turned it into the highest rated talk show in Chicago. She quickly got over their words as her show eventually became one of the biggest hits of the 20th century.

Which words have been spoken over you in the past and are affecting your ability to dream and to go after God's greatest plan for your life?

You believe yourself more than anyone. That's why you must start filling your mind and filling your mouth with God's word over you. You have to start hearing the word of God and then speaking positive confessions over yourself.

"What you repeatedly hear, you eventually believe."
– Mike Murdock

4. People.

Satan will strategically use other people to distract you from the plan of God for your life. A very clear Bible illustration of wrong soul ties is in the life of Samson. Delilah was a distraction sent from Satan to steal the power of God from his life.

Delilah did not believe like him. His family did not approve of her. She wasn't from the same heritage. But what did Samson say of her? "She pleases me well" (Judges 14:3, *NKJV*).

In other words, she was pleasing to look at. She was attractive. Be warned when your eyes lead you astray from God's plan for your life. It is a trap that leads to great regret. Samson allowed his eyes to lead him away from God's plan.

Think about it. Samson is still considered the strongest man who ever lived, but he went down in history for his weakness: Delilah. At the end of his life, this mighty man of God was left blind, weak and power-less in the enemy's camp. Why? Distractions that came from a wrong soul tie.

This is an analogy of what can happen to us when we allow a person to distract us from God's original plan. If there is someone in your life who is a distraction sent from Satan to get your eyes off the plan of God for your life, get them out of your life!

Recognize it. You will feel inside, how Samson became outside — chained, bound, and powerless to defeat this enemy. If you don't have peace deep down inside that God approves of this relationship or this influence, *run!* Don't fool yourself. Don't justify it because of what your feelings are trying to convince you.

5. Money.

Satan will do his best to convince you that you will never have enough money to fulfill your dreams. "You will never have the money you need. Accept it. God is not going to bless you. He hasn't yet and he won't!" He'll say.

He is a liar. He is incapable of telling the truth (John 8:44)!

He will bring up your past. Perhaps, you filed bankruptcy. You are in debt. You have had financial difficulties and struggles for years. You don't have any extra money to start that business or to go back to school or to get that car.

It has been reported that Walt Disney filed bankruptcy seven times. He was rejected by 301 banks. Did he let that stop him? No! Why? He stayed focused on his dreams no matter what.

If you do not have what you need to pursue your dreams, make it a seed. God can multiply seed sown. He can't multiply money sitting in your pocket. If you are down to your last dollar, don't spend it, give it. Invest in your dreams. Believe God for the impossible.

> Stop remembering what God has forgotten.

Where there's vision, there's provision.

6. Your past.

Have you ever noticed that as soon as you start to get a little hope on the inside of you that maybe God can still use you, suddenly, Satan starts reminding you of your past? It's not coincidental.

He works tirelessly to remind you of how bad you have been, how much you don't deserve anything, how guilty you are, how worthless you are! He is the Accuser of the Brethren (see Rev. 12:10).

I can just imagine him carrying around his notebook of all of our sins recorded. He is a copious notetaker. He records every wrong thing you and I have done and he does not forget it—nor does he let us. Remember, his job is to distract you from your dreams. If reminding you of your past will stop you from dreaming, then you can count on it, he will do it.

Catch on to his tricks. Rip up the notebook and put it behind you.

That's why Paul said, "This *one thing* I do, forgetting those things which are behind, and reaching to those things which are before, I press toward the mark for the prize of the high calling of God in Christ Jesus" (Phil. 3:13-14, *KJV*, emphasis added).

Paul knew that if he was going to fulfill what God wanted him to do, it would require that he let go of the past and hang on to a dream. You have to forgive yourself and receive God's forgiveness if you are ever going to reach your dreams.

Stop remembering what God has forgotten. Your sins. Your mistakes. Your past.

7. Disappointments.

The dream-thief, Satan, will use disappointments, let downs and failures to discourage you from ever stepping out again.

Thomas Edison said, "I failed my way to success". We will make mistakes. That is just part of growing. So many people focus on the mistake and can't seem to get past it.

Did you know that Madonna dropped out of college and moved to New York hoping to find fame? While she was struggling financially, she was hired at Dunkin' Donuts in Times Square and didn't even last a day. After squirting jelly filling all over a customer, she was fired. This *Material Girl* went through several fast food jobs before she was introduced to the rock music scene in 1979 and has become a entertainment legend. She didn't let a series of disappointments stop her from her dreams.

How many disappointments have you had?

If you have an American penny nearby, you should take a good look at the face of Abraham Lincoln and let his life inspire you no matter how many disappointments you have faced.

Did you know that Abraham Lincoln was faced with many, many opportunities to give up on his dream of being president of the United States?

At 22 years old, he failed in business.

One year later, he ran for legislature and lost.

At 24 years old, he experienced a second business failure.

At 26 years old, he lost the woman he loved. She died.

The next year, he suffered a nervous breakdown.

At 29 years old, he lost another political race.

At 34, he made an unsuccessful run for Congress.

At 37, he did get elected to Congress, only to be defeated again
two years later.
At 46, he lost his bid for the Senate.
The next year, he failed in his attempt to become vice president.
At 49, he was defeated for the Senate again.
He had four sons, but only one lived to adulthood.
At 51 years old, Abraham Lincoln was elected President of the
United States and successfully led the country through one of
its most difficult periods.

Many people would have said, "No way," but not Lincoln. He fought
for his dream no matter how many previous disappointments he faced!

"A dream comes about with much business and painful effort"
(Ecc. 5:3, *AMP*).

Pick Yourself Up!

Your enemy would love for you to develop a victim mentality. He wants
you to think that you are the only one going through what you're going through. Keith Moore says, "Don't ever, ever, ever...never, never,

never...ever...feel sorry for yourself."

Why? Warfare always surrounds the birth of a miracle!

We all face storms. We all face discouragement and disappointments from time to time. Where does most of our growing take place? In the storms of life. I truly hate some of the things I've been through in my life. I wish more than anything I had made different choices and resisted temptations. I wish I could erase many things from my past, but I would not be who I am today and I certainly would not know God the way I know Him now if I hadn't gone through those hard places.

I want you to stop focusing on what you're leaving and zero in on what you're going toward. You are going to be more fulfilled than you've ever been in your life. With God ordering your steps, you're going to pull your shoulders back, hold your head up and walk right into His perfect will for your life.

Always remember that three steps forward and two steps back still equals one step ahead.

"Don't ever, ever, ever...never, never, never...ever...feel sorry for yourself."

"I've finally received my rescue."

I had the privilege of hearing you speak at my church recently. I am a single mother of an 18 year old that is leaving for the Air Force in November. Last August I became engaged to someone I have loved since I was 17 years old, I am now 40. One month to the day before our wedding, the very night we had finished marriage counseling with our pastors he allowed himself to be put in a situation of indiscretion. I called off the wedding and told him to move out of my house. I had allowed him to move in just a few weeks prior. I justified the whole situation…I was 40 and I could handle what ever came along with my decisions. I later allowed myself to become involved with him again thru a long distance relationship.

Just 2 weeks before your visit to my church someone loaned me your series on Breaking Soul Ties. I would not listen to it because I knew I wasn't ready. Yesterday I began "hearing" the Word the way you recommended in your message on Sunday. I chose your CDs to listen to on Breaking Soul Ties. I know that this is not an easy journey, but it is the journey I have chosen. I want to get back to the place with God that I know I belong and even go beyond that into a deeper relationship with Him. Please pray for me and know that if you didn't come to my church for any other reason God sent you for me. I feel like the story where the guy was stranded on the roof of his house during the flood and he kept refusing help that came his way because he said that God was going to send someone. When he died and went to Heaven he asked why God didn't deliver him and he was told that God sent a boat, a helicopter and a raft…what more do you want? God has been dealing with me for a while and I finally received my rescue. Thank you so much for your life and ministry.

- Chera

Chapter 8

Stronger Today
Than Yesterday

You must have *daily* doses of God's Word in order to develop the strength to sever any ungodly soul tie, especially a sexual soul tie. You cannot do this on your own. That's why you need the power of God's Word going into your spirit and building you up daily. Remember, nobody can make you make the right decisions. Only you can make the decision for your life.

So, how do you build your faith? Or how does faith grow? The number one method God has given us to increase our faith is found in Romans 10:17. "So then faith comes by hearing and hearing by the Word of God" (*NKJV*). Faith will grow as you spend time hearing God's Word. That's easy. Every time you listen to a faith-building message, your faith grows. But just as faith comes by hearing, faith also goes by not hearing.

We have all been given *the measure* of faith (Rom. 12:3, *KJV*). Just like we all were born with the same amount of muscles. The only difference between my muscles and those of a champion weight lifter is that their muscles have been developed more than mine.

It works the same way in the spirit. The more your faith grows and develops, the more you can handle. That's why you see some people believing for millions of dollars and others believing for gas money. One has developed their faith to a greater degree.

Simply by choosing to hear a message from the Word of God on CD or on your iPod at some point in your day will play a strategic part in your plan to be free. Remember, the reason the Word is so important during this time of breaking soul ties is because ungodly soul ties lead to *confusion, misery, torment and disobedience.*

When your soul has become tied to another person through the principles of sin, you have literally opened yourself up to the lies of Satan. He is working hard to keep you locked in this situation, hoping to destroy your life.

Hearing God's Word, the Truth, must be a priority in your *daily* schedule. God's truth will override Satan's lies. And it won't be over-night. It takes hearing the Truth over and over and over until you think you could scream because you're so tired of hearing it, but you do it again and again and again.

What you must realize is that you are *gaining inner strength* to help you break free. You may not see yourself getting stronger. You may feel just as connected to that person as you always have been, but some-thing is happening inside of you. And if you keep it up, you will break free.

If you want to be free and full of vision, you have to turn it up a notch in your daily routines and disciplines. I am absolutely, positively, 100% convinced that your daily routine will lead you into God's plan or away from it. It's what you do on a daily basis that counts.

"The secret of your future is hidden in your daily routine."
- Mike Murdock

Set yourself up to succeed.

"Daily? I don't have time, Terri." I think you might. Did you know that the average American watches six hours of TV each day? By the time you are 60 yrs old, you will have wasted 15 years of your life sitting in front of a television watching other people pursue their dreams. That's a quarter of your life. What if you eliminated just one hour of TV each day? That would create 365 hours of additional time each year. To do what? Build your faith. Grow. Move on with your life. Prepare for your dreams.

The average person commutes 30 minutes each way to and from work. In five years, that's 1,250 hours in the car or enough to give yourself the equivalent of a college education. We have the time to build our faith by hearing the Word, we just have to seize the opportunities.

Once I began to make a habit of listening to faith-building messages every single day, that's when I began to change. And it wasn't hard to start this habit. I simply took my CD player in my bathroom, wrote a big sticky note that said "Push play" and stuck it on my mirror. On day one, I pushed the button and began a habit that changed my entire life.

I began to think beyond my present circumstances. I began to think bigger. I began to fall in love with God, with myself again and with my future. God has so much for you to do, but you can't do it until your faith is developed to such a degree that you *simply believe* all things are possible.

Psalm 119:130 (*NKJV*) says that the entrance of God's Word brings light. When a person is wounded physically, doctors usually put things under the light to see the real problem. When a light turns on, you see things you couldn't see when you were in the dark. You may be in the dark about your emotional wounds. You may not be able to see what's going on in you. God's Word will reveal any darkness in your soul. His Word is the cure for the insecure, the broken, the wounded, the bruised inside.

It was when I developed a *daily plan* to hear God's Word that I began to see things I never saw before about myself, my insecurities, my past, my patterns in relationships, my weaknesses, etc. God's Word literally opened my eyes to the truth.

Just push play

Get on a quest to hear the Word of God at some point each day. I highly encourage you to invest in some faith-building messages. You can go online and order some, download some today for your iPod or MP3 player, borrow some from a friend, but do something immediately.

Set yourself up to succeed. Place the CD player or whatever device you prefer, in your bathroom the night before. All you have to do tomorrow morning is push play. Remind yourself with a note like I did if you have to. Put some CDs in your car so you can get built up during your commute tomorrow. Or carry your player into the kitchen while you are cooking or loading the dishwasher. You can take it to the laundry room while you are folding clothes or during your morning jog. Remember, every time you hear the Word, you're getting stronger.

Guess what? You will begin to desire more. Your spirit will actually crave to hear the Word. You will feel so alive on the inside. You will begin to feel the changes taking place on the inside. I receive countless testimonies of people who have started and maintained this discipline in their daily routine and vow to never quit because of the joy it has brought to their spirits.

Start with a 21 day goal to listen to the Word at some point during your day, even if it's for 10 minutes, just do something.

Read this verse from Psalms Now, chapter 17-18:

"I cry to You out of desperation, my God. Help me feel good about myself and about my role in Your service. Reveal Yourself in some special way this night that I may rest in joy and peace.

It's no wonder that I love You, God. You have granted me a security that I could never find among the things of this world. The traumatic experiences of this life cannot destroy me. You are never out of reach but are ever aware of my problems and conflicts.

And this is the God who is concerned about me. He reaches into my distraught life to heal my wounds. He encompasses me with eternal love. He surrounds me with His strength and

clothes me with His grace. He has given meaning to (my) life"
(emphasis added).

Imagine reading this daily until you are absolutely convinced that
it's true. That's what you have to do in order to get well. You study it. You
meditate on one verse. It's not about reading the whole Bible through in
a year, unless that's what you feel you need to do. It's about meditating
on one Scripture at a time until it gets down on the inside of you.

"The righteous cry out, and the Lord hears them; he delivers them
from all their troubles. The Lord is close to the brokenhearted and saves
those who are crushed in spirit" (Ps. 34:18, *NIV*).

Break it apart and personalize this verse:

"You hear me, Lord. You're right here in my kitchen, in my
den, in my bedroom with me.
I am crushed inside, Father, but you said you would save me. I
trust you, Lord."

It's *up to you* to seek healing in your life. You have to make an investment in your freedom and your healing. I did. I remember purchasing $60 worth of faith-building CDs online, and I couldn't believe I was spending so much money on the Word. Then I thought, "I would easily spend that much on a new outfit. This is my freedom we're talking about!"

What is healing worth to you? What are you willing to invest in now so that you can get well? Get your hands on as many faith-building messages as you can—especially ones that deal with emotional healing, freedom, confidence, faith, and dreams.

> The secret of your future is hidden in your daily agenda.

How much or how little you hear the Word depends on how soon you want to see results in your life. Joshua 1:8 says, "This book of the law shall not depart out of your mouth, but you shall meditate on it day and night" (*ESV*).

Day and night? Yes.

Don't skip a day. Don't skip a day. Don't skip a day without taking the medicine of God's Word that will bring healing. You are reading from a girl who was filled with insecurities, inferiorities, untreated wounds, brokenness, hiding it all under a wealth of activity and a big smile.

It wasn't until I got serious about hearing God's Word daily that I began to change. And I'm still changing. But it started one day at a time.

I haven't changed by one miraculous encounter. It's been little by little hearing God's Word every day, and not getting discouraged because it appeared nothing was changing. Little by little, my real smile returned. I began to laugh again. I began to dream again. Little by little, we change. The secret of your future is hidden in your daily agenda.

"If you want to see change in your life, change something you do daily."
– John Maxwell

You're getting stronger every day.

"God restored everything that was broken"

About a month and a half ago I finally cut an unhealthy relationship out of my life after 4 or 5 times of going back and forth leaving him and getting back together with him. I started dating him a little over a year ago and to make an extremely long story short, over the course of time that I dated him there were a lot of red flags that I saw. From this single relationship and choices that I made I fell into sin, felt guilt and shame, was verbally abused, manipulated, felt far away from God, my confidence and self-esteem decreased. I experienced anxiety, depression, insomnia, unforgiveness mainly towards myself, and pretty much wore a "mask" on my face hiding everything that was going on in the inside. There are things that I never told anybody and only brought to God as I prayed and continually read His Word. There were so many times that I would just drop to my knees and cry out to God as my worship music played in the background. It was as if this nightmare was never going to end.

Then one night I went on Youtube and I can't 100% remember what

I typed but I think it may have been soul ties and I clicked on your video. I had never heard about you or listened to your sermons. That night was the beginning of the road of transformation that God had set before me. I watched each of those videos in that one sitting, and I started to feel my heaviness begin to lift off of me. As days and days went by, I continued to watch your other podcasts and began taking notes and applying them to my life. I meditated on your messages and the Scriptures that you referenced. I felt such a connection with you and from hearing your own testimonies really felt like you understood what I was going through. Shortly after this, I got the strength to end the relationship. God started to confirm a lot of things to me about how I had been so deceived by the enemy. God did such an inner healing in me and restored everything that was broken. I was also able to finally forgive myself, leave my past behind, and later that guy and I forgave one another.

- Alanna

Chapter 9

"Can We Keep In Touch?"

Do you know how many former high school flames have popped back into each other's lives through Facebook? Some even twenty, thirty years later. The numbers continue to climb. Seems harmless to reconnect with old flames, see how they are doing and share a few memories, right? The statistics are rising continuously of those who not only got in touch but got in bed.

How does that saying go, "The road to hell is paved with good intentions"? There really is some truth to that. We have such a unique ability to justify staying in touch. We reason with ourselves why it's not that bad to just be friends with a former love. "What's so wrong with emailing each other?" It's not that it's so bad or so wrong, it's that you were deceived once by this wrong soul tie, and you can be deceived again. "A little leaven leavens the whole lump" (Gal. 5:9, *ESV*).

Modern technology has made it more difficult to completely sever ties with old relationships. It's nothing to stumble across a photo of him/her online or to nonchalantly send them a quick text in those lonely moments.

As I was researching statistics for this book, I googled "Facebook affairs" and discovered a comment from someone in an affair recovery group saying that she realized more and more that connections made through social networking blossomed into an affair. Many times the affairs grew out of new relationships nurtured online, but more often they developed as a result of reconnections with past friends or lovers.

Another site stated bluntly that unless you're single, divorced or widowed, don't look up that old flame. Why? It leads to danger. Researchers interviewed married men and women who rationalized getting in touch with an old love through social networking. They considered it private, harmless and safe when they hit send. In fact, 62% of the married couples wound up having an affair for which none of them began the contact with that in mind.

"Keep me from the snares they have laid for me, and from the traps of the workers of iniquity" (Ps. 141:9, *NKJV*).

Whether or not you stay in touch with a former soul tie is up to your unique situation; however, you need to be honest about what God is speaking to your spirit. If you have to hide this interaction from someone, then it's wrong. Anything we have to keep hidden has power over us. Satan loves to have power over us.

Imagine leaving your Facebook account open for your spouse to access any time. Does that make you feel uncomfortable or fearful? If you have nothing to hide, it shouldn't matter. Whether you're married or not, but you find yourself constantly checking on a former soul tie obsessively, delete them. "No, Terri! I can't do that!" Hey, if you can't see what they're doing, you won't be tempted to stalk them. You need to take every measure you can to break free from this wrong attachment to your soul.

In Beth Moore's powerful book, <u>When Godly People Do Ungodly Things</u>, she parallels this bondage in wrong relationships to the serpent corrupting and seducing Eve in the book of Genesis like a poison or a venom. She instructs those seeking restoration to detoxify. In order to detoxify, you must cut yourself off from the source or sources and all other connections to the source," says Moore. "You may really need some stiff accountability to accomplish this detoxification, but it is vital that you do."

If you've been involved in an extramarital affair or sex before marriage, you need to do everything you can to cut off all forms of contact. Don't justify the text messaging. Don't reason with yourself that you can be alone and nothing will happen. As Beth Moore puts it, "Don't rationalize a friendship! Too many have tried, only to stay deceived on one level or another."

Wean yourself

Psalm 131:2 says, "Surely I have calmed and quieted my soul; like a weaned child with his mother. Like a weaned child is my soul within me ceased from fretting" (*AMP*).

You literally have to wean yourself from that person to whom you have ungodly soul ties. To wean means to deprive. You have to deprive yourself of this wrong soul tie until you no longer desire them.

We see the weaning process most commonly with nursing mothers. When she is ready to wean that child from the breast or bottle or even a pacifier, there will be some screaming that takes place. It's not an easy process in most cases. You are literally removing from that baby what he/she is used to having. When things are taken from us, we don't respond favorably. Notice, it is a process.

Each day it becomes a little more manageable. Some days seem like utter torture hearing the screams and cries for what they are used to receiving. Your soul will respond in like manner. Your mind, your will and your emotions your soul—will absolutely throw a fit. Your mind will convince you that you cannot do this. Your will will work against you. Your emotions will be haywire. You cannot trust your feelings at this stage.

This is when hearing the Word of God is of utmost importance. You must consciously and routinely hear faith-building messages that strengthen your mind, your will and your emotions. You cannot fight this battle alone.

I want you to read this and retain it: *when you deny yourself that person, you are not rejecting them; you are rejecting sin.* There's a big difference.

Read that short paragraph again.

Satan would love to make you feel mean, cold-hearted, ruthless and borderline evil for saying "No" to this ungodly contact in your life, but he is a liar. You are doing the right thing by not staying in sin. You cannot remain in sin and be used of God. You cannot stay in sin and be in God's perfect will for your life. Period.

One of the first feelings you will have when you finally break it off is fear. The fear of never recovering, the fear of future cirumstances, the fear of heartbreak, the fear of moving on. You will need to cling to God as never before.

Focus on scriptures that bring comfort and peace to your mind.

Read them over and over until they get down on the inside of you. Take it a step further by speaking them out loud out of your own mouth. You need to hear yourself speaking God's promises over your mind and your soul.

"Though I walk in the midst of trouble, You will revive me; You will stretch forth Your hand against the wrath of my enemies, and Your right hand will save me. The Lord will perfect that which concerns me; Your mercy and loving-kindness, O Lord, endure forever—forsake not the works of Your own hands" (Ps. 138:7-8, *AMP*).

Isn't that encouraging? God will revive you. What does that mean?

· To bring back to life or consciousness; resuscitate
· To impart new health, vigor, or spirit to
· To restore to use

Hey, could you use some of that? Then, call on God more than ever before.

Do not feel ashamed to talk with Him about what you're feeling. Be honest. He already knows anyway; so talk to Him about it. He said that He will perfect that which concerns you. Does this situation concern you? Are you troubled by it? Are you confused? Are you afraid? God will make it perfect.

Trust God with all your heart to empower you with a divine strength you've not known or experienced before. This strength will enable you to not melt like a puddle when those feelings begin to surface. No, you will rise to the occasion and stay focused on where you're headed.

"When I walk into the thick of trouble, keep me alive in the angry turmoil. With one hand strike my foes, With your other hand save me. Finish what you started in me, God. Your love is eternal—don't quit on me now" (Psa. 138:7-8, *THE MESSAGE*).

God wants to finish what He started in you. It's never too late. Let the finishing start. Remember, whatever God desires to remove from your life is ultimately for your benefit. He would never withhold something good from you. He is a good God and a loving Father. If He wants something or someone removed, He sees something down the road that you can't see yet. Trust Him. He's always right.

Make a plan

My marriage counselor instructed me years ago with five little words, that they changed my life: *Fight fear with a plan.* You need a plan. Consciously think of what you're going to do when:

· You walk in your empty house on a Friday night with nothing to do
· You receive a text from them inviting you to come over
· Your phone is continuously ringing
· You run into them
· Your friends update you on them
· You see pictures of them online
· You begin to sink into depression
· You miss them
· Your mind is replaying memories

This is reality. You need a plan for when these situations occur. In the following chapters, I am going to offer you some practical plans to get your mind off that person and onto your purpose. You will feel in control of your emotions, peace in your surroundings and health in your finances and body.

> The decisions you are making today will affect someone else's life.

Look Down the Road

Determine to press through whatever God's telling you to do, trusting that down the road, you are headed for more peace than you've ever had in your life.

You've probably heard the phrase: "A wise person does today what they will be happy with tomorrow. A foolish person does what feels good today and ends up regretting it tomorrow." How true that is.

Eating sugar and all the candy you want is fun, but having a complete root canal hurts! We always end up paying for the foolishness of today somewhere down the road. Many people say, "Play now and pay later!" I've discovered in my life that there is a price we pay to be in the will of God and it's spelled: P-A-I-N. You might be wondering, "Exactly how is this supposed to motivate me?" I'm getting there.

Anytime God is getting ready to advance your instructions or move you into a new phase in your life, it requires another step of obedience. And many times, it requires doing something that our flesh simply does not want to do. It hurts. It doesn't feel good. It creates a fight between our flesh and our spirit. But it's always for our good. God sees things that we don't see, and there is a divine reason He wants you to get victory in those areas where you've suffered repeated failure.

For example, God may be getting ready to do a new thing in your life, to promote you, to move you into a new area of ministry, but He's dealing with you about forgiving someone who hurt you years ago. You know you must, but it hurts. Somehow it feels good to hold on to that debt they owe you. Or God may be telling you that it's time to confront this person who has intimidated you for far too long. If this person has had a great amount of power over you in the past, then it's not going to just go away without a fight. A flesh and spirit fight.

In the example of Jesus in the Garden, we see Him battling between doing what He knew was right and what He wanted to do. His flesh was crying out. He knew it was going to be a pain beyond human comprehension. He didn't want to do it, but He could see down the road. If He could press through the pain, if He could endure the pain of the cross and keep His eyes focused on the resurrection, He would have an amazing life beyond human comprehension. He would be in the perfect will of God. He would have fulfilled His assignment. One day, He would have no pain, He would be seated at the right hand of the Father, and have an eternity of joy. And He did it.

And look how His obedience affected eternity. It affected generations. It affected you personally! Isn't it amazing to think that *somebody in need is waiting on the other side of your obedience?* The decisions you are making today, as painful as they may be right now, will affect someone else's life. Whatever you are struggling with to be in the perfect will of God, your decision will affect the lives of others.

Look down the road. Don't quit now. Don't give in to that temptation. Don't be intimidated by it anymore. Press through with everything in you and you will not regret it.

Psalm 118:5 says, "In my anguish I cried to the Lord, and he answered by setting me free" (*NIV*). How many times have I confessed that?

Determine to press through whatever God's telling you to do. Trust Him knowing that down the road, you are headed for more peace than you've ever had in your life. You will be highly favored and promoted because of your obedience. You will be prosperous and successful because of your willingness to endure the pain that your flesh feels while it's not getting its way. Don't look at just what's in front of you—look beyond what you see with your eyes. Look further. Be assured that whatever God is telling you to get out of your life, to do away with, to forgive, to be patient, it's so that He can do a new thing in your life. The pain will go away.

The truth is: you will never, ever, ever, ever be happy outside of God's will for your life. So you might as well stop delaying His plan for your life because of how painful it is right now.

God wants to use you. But He can't use you publicly until you've gotten victory privately. When you defeat these wrong soul ties that have controlled you in the past, when you look down the road at the peace, the joy and success God promises you will have…get ready! You will look back over your life and say, "I am so glad I did what I did to get to where I'm at. I'm not even the same person I used to be!"

> "A wise person does today what they will be happy with tomorrow."

"I love that you have begun this teaching. I have never heard of anyone teaching these crucial concepts. I came to Christ at the age of 30 years old, after many negative soul ties had been knitted to my soul. That has been 20 years and to this day I so desire to be free from the bondage of past unhealthy relationships. I thank you and especially our Lord Jesus Christ for this teaching as it will serve to set many captives free, including me! Today is a new day for me to walk in freedom; it marks a turning point in my life! May the Lord continue to richly bless you as you faithfully serve Him."

- Elizabeth

Chapter 10

Declutter the Memories

Clutter literally blocks your ability to move ahead. You've heard the phrase, "A cluttered desk is the sign of a cluttered mind." We need to de-clutter your environment because in essence, it effects your emotional health.

You may have reminders of your past just laying around your house and you have no idea what those things are doing to your emotions. Satan works through our five physical senses. He uses our sense of sight, sense of hearing, sense of touch, sense of taste and sense of smell to tempt us to go back.

- Cologne or perfume – one smell and you're ready to call them
- Letters – reminding you of just how deeply you felt for each other
- Gifts – remembering the thought put into what he/she gave you
- Lingerie – takes your mind places you don't need to be going
- Jewelry – the value of what he/she spent on you reminds you of how much you loved each other
- Music – every time you listen to "your song," it takes you

back in your mind to specific places and memories

- Photos – keeping the memories alive every time you look at those old pictures
- Emails and texts – holding on to these words keeps you held in your past
- Clothing – certain pieces of clothing make you think of them

"Do not bring a detestable thing into your house or you, like it, will be set apart for destruction" (Deu. 7:26, *NIV*).

This does not mean that every single reminder of your past needs to be destroyed – only those that have a negative emotional attachment to you. You know which things they are. If you look at that photo and it causes you to spiral backwards in your mind and you begin feeling anxiety, sadness, grief and hopelessness, toss it.

I'm not going to say it's easy. It will be hard at first. Your flesh will want to hang on to all those reminders and mementos. It may take a few rounds of cleaning before you actually come to the point of truly ridding yourself of negative memorabilia from old soul ties. Each time you clean it out, you're getting stronger and clearing your mind for the new things God is waiting to give you. That's a great incentive.

Stormie Omartian writes, "The less contact you have with what is not of God, the more of God you can have in your life, and the more you will know His love, peace, joy, healing and wholeness."

In addition to tossing negative attachments, you should also set a goal to simply declutter your environment from all messes. The benefits are amazing. You will experience a new level of peace simply from cleaning up and cleaning out.

I recently received an email that said:

"A month ago, I moved out of my parent's home that looked like the chaos of seven very strong minded, lazy and troubled people living together. The house was like this since we were young kids. Now that I'm on my own there is a calmness in cleanliness. In fact, I see now that the most troubled people in my family have the dirtiest dwellings. I still have things in boxes (I have almost no furniture) but there is no more of that heart sinking depression that comes from being dirty."

"I will walk within my house with a perfect heart" (Ps. 101:2, *NKJV*).

A peaceful home leads to a peaceful mind. When you start to care about your surroundings, it's a sign you're starting to care about yourself.

Clean the mess

> Clutter and disorder cause a lack of peace, confusion, and waste time.

I love the story in John 5 of the guy laying by the pool of Bethesda. For 38 years, he had been waiting for someone to pick him up and put him in the pool so he could be healed. When Jesus came along and saw that he had been laying in that condition for so long, He asked him, "Do you want to become well? Are you really in earnest about getting well?"

Isn't it interesting that Jesus had to ask him, "Are you sure you want to get well?" In other words, "Are you just satisfied with this life? Are you content just waiting for somebody to come along and pick you up?"

The invalid said, "Sir. I have nobody when the water is moving to put me into the pool; but while I am trying to come into it myself, somebody else always steps down ahead of me."

Jesus said to him, "Get up! Pick up your bed (sleeping pad) and walk!"

Jesus gave the command, "You've been laying around wallowing in self-pity, complaining, passive, doing nothing. It's time to get up and not only that—make up that bed, clean up your mess you've been laying around in, and get movin. Get on with the call of God on your life. Time is wasting. You've got things to do. Don't waste any more days of your life just waiting on somebody else to come encourage you. *You get up. You clean up. You get moving!*" (Terri's paraphrase)

Verse 9 says, "Instantly, the man became well and recovered his strength *and picked up* his bed and walked" (*AMP*, emphasis added). God may be telling you the same thing. It's time to clean up. Clean yourself up and clean up your environment. I believe this process will also prepare you for promotion. Right now God is preparing you to move into the next thing He has for you. And I want to help you step into this promotion. I want you to get a vision to clean.

It's been said that the way you do *anything* is the way you do *everything*. That means if your house, car, or office is a disorganized mess, your life and your mind *could be* a disorganized mess too.

Imagine how your life would be different if it were more organized. Perhaps you would reduce the amount of times you are late or your bills are paid late, you would waste less time looking for things, you would spend less money replacing items you can't find, you would experience a new level of peace in your home. Beyond all of those benefits, I believe you are also positioning yourself to receive more blessings from God. When you are faithful over the things you have, God can give you more.

If we are honest with ourselves, we can acknowledge the side-effects that come from a cluttered life. Clutter will cause you to feel overwhelmed, it robs your energy, costs money, takes away the peace and beauty of your home, and simply makes life harder. Paul instructs us in 1 Corinthians 14:40 to, "Let all things be done decently and in order" (*NKJV*, emphasis added).

It is really difficult to be successful with what God has entrusted to us when we are not organized. Why? Clutter and disorder cause a lack of peace, confusion, and waste time.

> Take care of what you have and God will begin to bless you with better.

This is a profound principle that can change your life: *Finish what you start and take care of what you have* and God will bless you with better. I like to say that doing so will prepare you for promotion.

Matthew 25:21 says, "You have been faithful with a few things; I will put you in charge of many things" (*NIV*). New American Standard says, "Because you were loyal with small things, I will let you care for much greater things" (emphasis added).

Finish Your Laundry

Years ago when my parents had no money—I mean they were believing God to put food on the table, driving a car with 200,000 miles on it—my mom learned a profound principle that absolutely changed her life. This principle put us on a course that helped us become more successful and more blessed than ever.

This turning point came from three simple words: Finish your laundry. That's it. Finish your laundry. The principle that God was revealing to her was this: *Finish what you start and take care of what you have, then I can bless you with better.*

Mom says that when they were going through this time of lack and insufficiency in their lives, she got into a habit of never really finishing the laundry. She would wash the clothes, dry the clothes, and then put them all in a big pile and throw them on the guest-room bed.

She would leave them in the guest bedroom all week, two weeks, or even longer. If she needed anything, she would go into the guestroom and grab the clothes or the towels she needed for the day.

Until one day while she was in there pulling something out of the pile, she heard the Lord say, "Finish your laundry." And she thought, *What's the big deal about finishing my laundry?* And the Lord began to teach her to finish what she starts and take care of what she has.

The laundry wasn't finished just because it was washed, dried, and thrown into a big pile. The Lord taught her to actually take the towels, fold them up, and put them away. He instructed her to iron the clothes, hang them on the hanger and take them to the closet. That is finishing what you start. That's being faithful with small things.

It sounds pretty simple and basic, but it comes straight from the Word of God. As a result, my Mom went from wearing cut-down maternity dresses to designer suits. She went from driving an old beat-up car with bald tires to a brand new Cadillac. As she began practicing the habit of finishing what she started and taking care of what she had, then God began to bless her with better. Much better.

You could be believing God for a new car, but the one you have is so full of junk, the lining is ripped and hanging from the roof, French fries are stuck in the seats and straw wrappers and soda cans thrown on the floor. It hasn't been washed since 2008, but you're believing God for a new one.

Here's your solution to your breakthrough: Clean your car! Take care of what you have and God will begin to bless you with better. Empty out all the trash, wash those seats off, vacuum the floor, go get the car washed, do something! Show God that you can be trusted with small things and that you're going to honor Him with what you have. Eventually, He will bless you with better things.

Are you the type of person who gets really excited about new ideas, new projects, new goals, but then loses enthusiasm and ends up with several half-finished projects?

Perhaps you started to learn a foreign language. You spent $450 on the language course, practiced every day for two weeks and then stopped. It's been months now and all you can say in French is "Ou sont les toilettes?" (Where are the toilets?)

Maybe you went to a scrapbooking party. You Spent $350 on papers, die-cuts, stickers and a 12 x 12 photo album. You got inspired. You completed one page that took you three days, and never finished the scrapbook.

Did you start a Zumba class? You loved it! Perhaps you felt a little crazy at first but then you got the hang of it. So, you signed up for a 12 month membership—since it was cheaper to do it that way. You went consistently for five weeks and now it's been four months. You feel fat. You wasted money. You're mad at yourself, but not so mad that you go back to the gym.

Maybe you were determined to write your book. You got started. You wrote the first chapter and half of chapter two. That was three years ago.

Remember this: 10 completed projects would be far greater than 20 half finished ones. I only know how to teach from experience. One year, I started writing a book in June. I worked on it for about three days nonstop hoping to have it written by the end of July. With all my traveling and speaking engagements, I had to stop. I kept thinking, I would pick it back up in August when I would be home a little more but I wasn't home a little more. I was gone more. So, I put it off.

Meanwhile, I had another book on my heart. So I started jotting down ideas for it every pocket of time I could find. I would be sitting on a plane, and I would write thoughts for this other book. It was going to be a small book so it shouldn't take too long to write. *I can do that quick!* I thought.

Then, I wanted to start a new notebook. So, I started working on that project. I actually finished about 75% of it, but then I was traveling and working on new messages nearly every week, so I had to put it on hold.

The results: three books in the works and *none completed*. Who is benefitting from these projects God put on my heart? No one.

Not only was no one benefitting from all these unfinished projects, but I was stressed out and uneasy inside because nothing was complete. It drained energy from me, discouraged me, and frustrated me. I kept feeling like this weight was on my shoulders and I didn't know what to do first.

James 1:8 says, "A doubleminded man is unstable in all his ways" (*KJV*). How many of his ways? All of them. Has anyone ever described you as unstable? Now, you know why! You're double-minded. You decide one way and do another. I understand. I was so frustrated that I just did nothing about it. You could be thinking, "Then why am I learning from you?" Because I found a solution!

Physical Space & Mental Space

When projects go unfinished, not only do they take up physical space, but they also take up mental space. All of your unfinished projects are draining your energy and stealing your peace.

"Let all things be done decently and in order" (1 Cor. 14:40, *NKJV*), Another translation says, "But let everything be done in a right and orderly way" (*NCV*).

Cleaning up your messes allows you to focus, with more energy, on the future. That's what you need to do now more than ever. You need to get your mind off the past and onto the future. So, let's get started by discovering where you have messes. Messes can be in your car, purse, closet, checkbook, desk, garage, kitchen, bills, bathroom, email inbox, or filing cabinet.

Clutter Clean-Out Step 1: Make a list of your physical messes.

I encourage you to take a walk through your home room-by-room. Get a sheet of paper or use your smart phone or iPad to make note of what needs to be cleaned in every room. Don't start cleaning yet, just begin by writing down the goal. Focus on one room at a time, and write everything you see that needs to be done.

You might ask, "Why is it so important that I clean my messes?" Remember, each mess robs you of your energy and steals your peace.

You also may have negative emotional reminders of your past that need to be thrown away. I'll leave that up to you.

Key phrases to remember:
Let all things be done properly and in an orderly manner (1 Cor. 14:40).
He who is faithful over little will be ruler over much (Matt. 25:23).
The way you do *anything* is the way you do *everything*.

If your bed is always half made, perhaps your music album will remain half recorded. It's a profound principle, but it's a habit that you can change.

Your list could read this way:
Master Bedroom:
Wash sheets
Pick up magazines from the floor
Wash clothes laying on chair
Hang clothes up

Clean off nightstand

Clean out nightstand drawers

Clean off clutter on top of dresser

Put new lightbulbs in lamp

Dust off the ceiling fan

Vacuum floor

Light candles

Spray air freshner

Clean out under the bed

Then go to the next room. It could be the kitchen. Write down everything that needs to be done. Get your vision on paper (Hab. 2:2).

Clutter Clean-Out Step 2: Designate a day to start.

I recommend today. You might say, "Terri, you have no idea how much needs to be done. I can't start today. I need an entire week to really do this!" So many times we procrastinate on important matters simply because we are waiting for the perfect time or a great amount of time. You don't need a full week or even a full day. Use the time you have. It will add up and you will see tremendous results in a short time.

Clutter Clean-Out Step 3: Give yourself 20 minutes.

Set your alarm or timer for 20 minutes and focus on only one room. Go for it. See what you can accomplish in 20 minutes. You will be surprised.

Start with the room in which you spend the most time, and start with the clutter that's visible to the eyes. In other words, don't start with inside the dresser drawers or cleaning out the refrigerator. Start with the pile of mail on the kitchen counter top or the clothes laying on the floor. Start with what can be seen. It will encourage you as you see progress and motivate you to finish.

For example, I just cleaned out my make-up drawer in less than 20 minutes. It was nothing big but it was nagging at me every time I opened that drawer to get make-up. I was so bothered by the fact that it was packed with old and new make up, broken cases, old mascara tubes, and full of junk that needed to be thrown out. I kept thinking that I need to find time to clean this out.

I set aside 20 minutes to just clean it out. I set the alarm on my phone before going to bed one night and went at it. I was able to get the drawer completely cleaned and now, I have peace.

When something needs to be done and you don't do it, it nags on you. It steals your energy and your peace. It may only take 20 minutes of focused attention to do it.

Many times, we put things off because we think we need an entire day to focus on this huge project, but when do you have an entire day for clutter clean-out? I rarely do. Give yourself 20 minutes and start today.

20 minutes X 30 days = 10 hours. And you won't even miss the 20 minutes.

Cleaning Out the Mental Clutter

Messes can be found anywhere. A mess can be even more than just physical surroundings. Bill Chandler defines a mess as *any disagreement between the way you desire your life to be and the way it actually is.*

Your weight could be a mess.

Your marriage could be a mess.

Your family relationships could be a mess.

Your emotions could be a mess.

Your career could be a mess.

Your finances could be a mess.

What is a mental mess? It is anything taking up space *in your mind* that is left unfinished.

It could be:
- A phone call that needs to be made
- An apology that needs to be said
- A relationship that needs to be severed
- A book that needs to be finished
- A degree that needs to be pursued
- A bill that needs to be paid off
- A promise that needs to be kept
- A thank you card that needs to be written
- A will that needs to be settled

This is clutter. Clutter makes you feel incomplete, embarrassed, annoyed, depressed, makes you feel bad and it robs you of your peace.

Successful People are Organized

I have noticed that the successful people I admire are not messy. They don't have clutter in their cars, on their desks, nor in their homes. I've seen a pattern here. Disorder causes a lack of peace. Clutter is disorder.

Imagine how you would feel if someone you greatly admire and respect asked for a ride in your car today. Would you be embarrassed about the condition of your car? Would you be honored to have them ride in your clean and nicely organized car?

Or what if your pastor made a surprise visit to your home tonight? When we are embarrassed about any condition of our lives it causes a lack of confidence. Remember, the way you do anything is the way you do everything.

Think of how good you feel when you walk in your house and it's all clean and in order. Doesn't it just bring peace? It just makes you feel good all around when your surroundings are in order. You can accomplish more of your goals when your clutter is cleaned up.

Why? Because your mind isn't pre-occupied with all that you *need to be doing*. It's done. You're at peace. Now, you can focus on the bigger picture. When we don't complete what we start or leave clutter in our lives, we aren't free to fully embrace the future. Just because we ignore something doesn't make it go away.

I was speaking in Canada one weekend and a sweet lady came up

> Ten completed projects have more power than twenty half-finished ones.

to me after my session and said, "Terri, what do I do? I have so many dreams and goals that it's overwhelming. I've been saying for years that I'm going to write five books. I'm going to record a music album. I'm going to write a play. I'm going to write a cookbook..." And the list went on. She said, "I've had these dreams my whole life and none of them have come true."

She kept saying, "I'm full of dreams!" She was probably in her 40's. I told her to start with one and dedicate 20 minutes a day to it until it's finished. I told her not to think about the other 15 projects she has on her heart to do. Just stay with that one for at least 20 minutes a day until it is done. Think of nothing else until you finish it.

She had a cluttered mind no different than a cluttered desk. She was overwhelmed by how much there was to do so she didn't do anything.

Years were going by and nothing was completed. Writing that one book will benefit her and others more than any of her dreams half done.

What could you do in 20 minutes?

Study a foreign language. Use your driving time to your advantage. The average person drives 20 minutes to and from work every day. Use that drive time to learn. Put your French CD in the car and parle francais. After one week of driving to work, that's close to two hours in your car learning, reaching a goal, fulfilling a dream!

Call a friend or relative that you've been procrastinating contacting during your commute home for 20 minutes.

Clean one room. Eliminate 20 minutes of television each night to dedicate to one room. Focus on that one room and one room alone until it's exactly the way you want it.

Read the Bible. Utilize the 20 minutes during your lunch break to build yourself up spiritually. Read one of the Proverbs for that day there are 31 Proverbs, so you could pick the chapter that matches the day of the week.

Pray. Instead of complaining about the hour you do not have, use the 20 minutes you do have and start your day off right. Spend some time praying for your family, your friends, your dreams and goals, or your peace of mind before you head off to work. Set your alarm to wake up 20 minutes earlier than usual.

Clean the dishes. Before you go to bed, set the alarm on your phone for 20 minutes to clean the kitchen. Load the dish washer. Wash off the counter tops. Go to bed in peace.

Write your book.

Practice your musical instrument.

Clean the refrigerator.

Clean out your purse.

Clean your car. Start a habit of emptying all the trash out of your car while you're pumping gas.

Exercise. Instead of waiting until you have that extra hour a day to work out, start with a 20 minute walk in your neighborhood. Go to the gym and walk on the treadmill for 20 minutes. It's better than no minutes! And remember, 20 minutes over the course of a month is 10 hours. That's some weight off your shoulders (and other places)!

5 Benefits to Getting Organized

1. Save money. Instead of buying things you've already have (like AA batteries, soap, glue, scissors, etc.), you will know exactly where to find them. You might actually make money selling things you don't need.

2. Save time. If your shoes always go in the closet (I know it's crazy!), you won't be running all over the house searching for them every time you're late for work.

3. Peace of mind. Your life will be less stressed and you will feel in control. It's peaceful when you know where things are. If you have any surprise visits, you're not humiliated by the condition of your home. You're confident to bring guests in. You have peace.

4. Focused energy. When you're not always feeling the pressure of needing to get that room cleaned up, you can focus your time and energy on the bigger goals of life—not the maintenance of life. You can really go after the dreams God has put in your heart.

5. Confidence. You will feel better about yourself when things are in order. Others develop confidence in you when they see your life seems to be in order. It just makes sense that you could be in line for a promotion.

When God sees that you are taking good care of what He's already given you, He is pleased and He is preparing your promotion. He will begin blessing you with better. Better dishes, better towels, better appliances, better clothes, better house, better car, better body, better job, better everything.

So what are you waiting for? Get your vision for your new clutter-free life by taking a few small steps today.

"You gave me hope"

"I just watched your Youtube video on soul ties and as soon as the video was over I came to your website. I'm breaking free from one and boy is it PAINFUL! But just finding you on Youtube and coming to your site gave me hope, and reassured me that this won't be an easy process, but I will make it through."

- Lanasia

Chapter 11

Save Your
Dollars and Sense

One of the greatest stress producers in our world is financial stress. It's one of the number of causes of divorce, anxiety, depression, and suicide. You might ask, "What does my financial reality have to do with breaking soul ties?" It has to do with you getting your life together and getting a vision to be in great financial shape. Perhaps you have been dependent on this person you have had a soul tie with financially. You need a vision. Whatever your situation is, I want you to have a vision for *your* finances.

You are where you are right now *financially* as a sum total of the decisions you have made to this point. However, the biggest push to change is being faced with reality. What is your *financial* reality?

Financial experts recommend that you have at least three months of your regular monthly expenses saved in an emergency savings account. In other words, if you lost your job or you had no consistent income, how long could you make it? Six months? Three months? One month? Until Friday?

If you were told that you had six months left to live, would you be satisfied with your financial condition? Would your family be taken care of? Would they have to sell the house? Pay off your debts? Borrow money?

I don't want this chapter to discourage you; I want it to inspire you to get a vision. Sometimes we need a good wake up call to realize something has to change. I know I did.

I'm only telling you to do what God instructed me to do as I began educating myself in personal finance. I got serious about being a good steward with the money God has given me. I got determined to make a difference for Jesus by financially supporting works and ministries I believe in.

As you are recovering from this soul tie that has been severed, you need to get a clear and compelling vision for your money. God said in His Word, "I wish above all things that you prosper and be in health, even as your soul prospers" (3 John 1:2, *NKJV*). God wants you blessed. Why? So you can be a blessing!

Having money doesn't necessarily make people happy, but owing money certainly can make you miserable. God wants you blessed and to owe no man anything but to love him!

Four Steps to a Healthy Financial Future

1. Picture your financial future

Stop looking at where you are and look at where you want to be financially. I am not a financial guru, but I do know that if you do not have a vision in any area of your life, that area will perish.

Napoleon Hill said, "I can teach anybody how to get what they truly want in life. I just can't find anybody who can tell me what they truly want."

How much money do you want to have saved within a year?
How much of your debt do you want paid off within a year?
How much does it cost to finance your dream or goal?
Do you have a clear vision of your financial future?

When Rodney and I were expecting our only child, Kassidi, we were believing God for a bigger house. We 'amazingly' saved $38,600 in five months! It was a lot of sweat, late nights and praying for opportunities to make money. But the most disappointing fact about that is this: after we raised that large amount of money for our house in five short months, years went by and we did not save one dollar. Why? Because a person with *no vision* will always return to their past.

We went right back to our old patterns of spending everything we earned. We had no vision. We had no focus. We had no financial goals.

And our finances were perishing (see Prov. 23:18).

God wants us to be wise with the finances He gives us. Proverbs 21:20 (*NLT*) tells us that a fool spends whatever he gets. Let's determine to stop playing like a fool and allowing Satan to distract us from our goals and our purpose. We should be so blessed that when God brings an opportunity across our path, we seize it. If we see a need, we meet it. God wants us to be able to publish the Gospel in foreign languages, finance mission trips and build safe houses for victims of human trafficking, but we can't if we spend everything we make and have nothing but debt to show for it. Read these startling facts of the *average* person from Dave Ramsey's book <u>The Total Money Makeover</u>:

- 43.7 million households in the U.S. have less than $1,000 in savings account.
- Nearly 60 million (1 in 5) have nothing in the bank.
- Wall Street Journal reports 70% of Americans live paycheck to paycheck.
- 80% of graduating college seniors have credit-card debt before they even have a job!
- 19% of the people who filed bankruptcy last year were college

students.

- Last year 6 billion credit card offers were put in our mail boxes, and we are taking advantage of those offers.
- According to CardTrak, Americans currently have $807 billion in credit card debt.

Weak desires bring weak results

As Christians, a great financial goal could be:

Tithe 10%

Save 10%

Live on 80%

What does that mean to you? What is 10% of your income? Do the math. That should be your goal to tithe every month. Deuteronomy 8:18 says, "But remember the Lord your God, for it is He who gives you the ability to produce wealth" (*NIV*).

Save money. Another great goal is to deposit 10% of your monthly income into your savings account every month. And live on the rest. That's vision.

That's a good assignment for you to do right now. Add up these numbers, and write them down. Habakkuk 2:2 says, "Write the vision and make it plain on tablets" (*NKJV*).

2. Add it up.

Establish a budget. Do you have an overview of your monthly income versus your monthly expenses? Do you know where your money is going? Gloria Steinem said, "We can tell our values by looking at our checkbook stubs."

Do you know what you earn? What do you bring home every month? What is your combined monthly income (if married)? You should be able to say instantly what you're monthly household income is. Write it down.

Do you know what you spend? You should be able to look at all of your monthly expenditures and know exactly how much you're spending. *Where is your money going?* You should be able to look at your monthly budget and know exactly where it's going.

"Most of us waste a lot of what we earn on 'small things'…we focus on the big-ticket items while ignoring the small daily expenses that drain away our cash." – David Bach, The Automatic Millionaire

Typically, the more we make, the more we spend. We waste so much money on small things and don't even realize it. David Bach says, "So many people say 'If only I could make more.'" Bach says, "But ask anyone who got a raise last year if their savings increased. In almost every case, the answer will be no."

Memorize this scripture taken straight from God's Word: Proverbs 21:20 "The wise have wealth and luxury, but fools spend whatever they get" (*NLT*).

One good tip to help you stop overspending is to practice using cash only. If you don't have the cash to get something, you don't get it. Give yourself a certain amount of cash each week to eat out, shop, get gas, everything. Put that cash in an envelope for the week. When the cash runs out, you eat at home. Period.

A study by Dunn & Bradstreet showed that credit-card users spend 12% to 18% more when using credit instead of cash. Dave Ramsey says, "It hurts when you spend cash, and therefore, you spend less!"

3. Yearn to be debt-free

How much debt do you have? Do you know? Is it so overwhelming that you've never taken the time to add it all up? I heard Creflo Dollar say, "What if Jesus Himself showed up in your living room tonight and asked, 'How much money do you need to get out of debt?' If you couldn't answer Him, you're not serious about getting out of debt."

Be honest with yourself. Do not be afraid to see that number. You need to target your faith towards a specific goal. This should be your highest goal: pay this debt off! Most financial experts recommend starting with your smallest debt. Put all extra money towards wiping out the smallest debt first. It will build momentum and inspire you to be completely debt-free. Don't buy what you don't have the money to buy.

Habakkuk 2:2-3: "Then the LORD told me: 'I will give you my message in the form of a vision. *Write it clearly enough to be read at a glance.* At the time I have decided, my words will come true. You can trust what I say about the future. It may take a long time, but keep on waiting—it will happen'" (*CEV*, emphasis added).

Place the vision somewhere in sight. Put it on your screen saver, on your phone, on your refrigerator, on the bathroom mirror, on your desk. Keep it in front of your eyes constantly. It helps you stay focused on this vision that you will be debt-free.

Once you've done the math for your financial goals, follow these 4 tips:

Goals must be in writing. If you don't have a copy of <u>My Personal Dreams & Goals Notebook</u>, you can order your copy at www.terri.com. I produced this notebook in order for you to see your vision on paper. "Thinking you can keep your goals in your head is just an excuse for not writing them down." – Author Unknown

Goals must be measurable. There's a big difference in saying, "I will pay more on my Visa card." and saying, "I will pay an extra $100 on my credit card within the next 30 days." Your goals must be measurable.

Goals must be realistic. If your goals are completely unrealistic, then you're setting yourself up for defeat. Be practical. Stretch yourself, but set goals that you fully believe you can reach.

Goals must have a deadline. Isn't it amazing how a deadline causes us to work much harder? Always answer the questions: how much and by when? How much money? By what date? It motivates you to work harder.

Consistency is the key to change. You get what you focus on. If you are serious about getting out of debt, you will. If you're serious about saving money, you will. "But Terri, I have no income. I have no extra money."

Ask the Lord for God-inspired ideas to earn money. I have friends, myself included, who have done some of the coolest things to reach their financial goals.

Bake cookies for model homes. I have a friend who baked cookies for builders showcasing model homes and was paid $.25 per cookie until she had the $4,000 she needed.

Breeding dogs. I have another friend who bred her dogs and made $3,000 for her financial goals.

Online sales. I have a friend who sells things online for herself and for others. She turned it into a fulltime business of selling things for others who either don't know how, don't have the time or don't want to bother. She makes 30% of sales, and has made thousands of dollars.

Sell old books. There are some places who want your old books and DVDs.

Photos. I have a friend who loves to take pictures and sells them online as a side income.

Pizza delivery. I have a friend who took an extra evening job delivering pizzas. Was it humbling when friends saw him driving around with the little pizza delivery sign on top of his car? Maybe so. But which is more rewarding? Being a little embarrassed to be seen by your friends or driving a debt-free car and building a savings account?

As Dave Ramsey says, "Change is painful!" Few people have the courage to seek out change. Most people won't change until the pain of where they are exceeds the pain of change. If you really get serious about getting out of debt, you will.

4. Educate yourself.

Hosea 4:6, "My people are destroyed for a lack of knowledge" (*KJV*). Good News Translation says it this way: *doomed because they do not acknowledge me.* That word *doomed* means *destined to fail or marked by an ill-fated future.* Ouch! Just not knowing what God wants you to do with your money could be your greatest downfall.

So, what's the solution? If you want to be skinny, study skinny people. If you want to be wealthy, study wealthy people. If you want to be successful, study successful people. Every success tip can be found in the Word of God. But we have to choose to educate ourselves.

I was reading (read those three words again) the book Rich Dad, Poor Dad about a wealthy woman whose home was burglarized. The thieves stole all the typical valuables around the house, jewelry, TVs, etc., but they left the most valuable things in her life: her books. The books are what educated her and taught her how to get wealthy; the thieves just didn't realize it.

Robert Kyosaki says, "Too many people are focused too much on money and not their greatest wealth, which is *their education*. Intelligence solves problems and produces money." He said, "The first thing you need to do is dig a deep hole and pour a strong foundation. Most people are trying to build an Empire State Building on a 6-inch slab."

When my husband married into my family, he was a new Christian. He was learning everything: how to believe God when it looked like nothing was happening, how to give when you have a need, how to walk in love when you're angry. Everything was foreign to him. But the one thing that seemed to confuse him or upset him more than anything was watching Christians just pray for God to bless them without doing anything!

He would say, "People are just expecting a giant check to show up in their mailbox." Even though Rodney believes that God can work financial miracles, he also believes that God gave us two hands and a brain to use. Faith without works is dead, right?

If we are spending everything we get, then why would God bless us with more? In many cases, more money will not solve our problems. It may actually accelerate the problem. Receiving an increase in cash could result in an increase in spending.

I had to begin educating myself in the area of money. You can spend all evening watching television or you can go in another room for 20 minutes and read a good book such as *The Total Money Makeover* by Dave Ramsey every night this month. Invest in yourself. Invest in change. Invest in your future.

If you want next year to be different than this year, then what steps are you going to take to make it different? So many people say, "Someday, I'm going to do that. Someday, I'm going to get serious about getting out of debt." Keep in mind, someday is not a day of the week. Time is going by. Debt is piling up. Money is being spent. Opportunities are being missed. Dreams are going unfulfilled.

One Christmas, I was driving around doing some shopping and listening to a financial expert in the car. In about 10 minutes of listening to his wisdom with money, I received the solution I needed to make a great financial decision. In 10 minutes!

You can do whatever you set your mind to do.
If you want to get out of debt, you will.
If you want to save $10,000, you will.
If you want to invest money, you will.

You just have to get determined that you're going to succeed on purpose! Someone once said, "You don't have to be great to get started but you have to get started to be great." Start where you are so that next year at this time, you will be one step closer to your financial dreams.

"My 22 year old son got involved with a girl who pulled him away from the Lord. I read your dad's devotionals daily and for some reason I clicked on your website for the first time. WOW! I heard your message on soul ties and had to email it to him. The Lord used you in such a powerful way! He has been delivered! Three years in bondage and he has been set free! Thank you Lord! Terri, I love your website you are such a great blessing and inspiration to me. I praise God for your ministry reaching young hearts! God bless you and your family richly and abundantly."

- Lucy

Chapter 12

What Are Your Clothes
Saying About You?

Let me start this chapter by "talking" with the women for a little bit. Did you ever take those fun quizzes in teen magazines that ask questions such as:

If you were a shoe, which would you be?

A. A sexy, strappy sandal

B. A running sneaker

C. A simple leather boot

D. A funky platform

Whose closet would you most like to raid?

A. Audrey Hepburn's

B. Julia Roberts'

C. Jennifer Lopez'

D. Pink's

These trivial questions are designed to pinpoint your unique sense of style. I have discovered that the way we dress says far more than we think.

Remember, we are communicating all the time without ever opening our mouths. Your unique clothing style says a lot about your personality. The way you dress communicates loudly into the minds of others who you are, what you represent, and what you want to convey. Coco Chanel once said, "If a woman is badly dressed, it's the dress we'll notice; but if she is impeccably dressed, it's the woman herself we'll notice."

Wearing a bold yellow hat with heavy make-up projects a different image than a baseball cap and ponytail. Your clothing style can speak volumes about you before you ever utter a word. What story do you think your outfit today told the world about you? Can they tell from your clothing choice today that you're depressed, you're going through something, you're athletic, you're motivated, you're successful, you're desperate, you're too busy to care?

Have you ever really thought about what message your clothing is projecting and what it says about you? When you leave the house in the morning or the evening, what are you and your outfit communicating? You might say, "I don't really care, Terri." Then, that's what you're communicating. Again you might say, "What does this have to do with me moving on from a hurtful relationship?" Volumes. Keep reading.

What is your clothing personality profile? (from All4Women.co.za)

The Classic: According to lamasbeauty.com, your clothing personality profile is classic if you don't like trendy clothes and prefer elegant, fashionable and dignified clothing.

These women are likely to be balanced, controlled, rational and emotional by nature. They don't like chaotic environments and are very caring and sincere.

The Romantics: The romantic profiles are sexy and curvy. Romantics look feminine by nature and are likely to have large eyes and soft rounded features.

These women prefer clothing which consists of rounded lines and dresses which have flowing shapes and waistlines. As with their looks, their style always has a sense of femininity. Women identified with this profile are charming, enchanting, arty and magnetic.

The Dramatic Personality: Women with dramatic personalities lean towards high-fashion and sophisticated looks. They wear severely tailored garments and prefer clothes with bright colors. They enjoy adding accessories to their outfits such as hats, belts, bags and elegant jewellery.

Dramatics tend to take control over situations, are prepared to take risks and they have natural authority. They are private persons and are always moving forward.

The Feminine: The ingénue clothing personality profile consists of women who like to wear frilly frocks, ruffles and lace. They're attracted to the Victorian look and prefer simple and feminine clothes. They add accessories like small jewelry, ribbons and cameos. These women are sweet, innocent and reflect pure femininity.

Keeping It Plain: The natural personality includes women who like to be plain (sporty). They don't want anything fussy or frilly and prefer garments with minimal details. Loose garments are part of their preferences as they're ideal for mobility.

The naturals accessorize with minimal jewelry such as simple chains, stud earrings and/or anything which is not over the top. In terms of their personality, they are warm-hearted people, responsible, friendly, enthusiastic and goal-orientated. They are good team players and very loyal towards friends.

The Sweeties: These women wear clothes with very fine detail. Their clothes usually have straight lines and beads here or there. They prefer jewelry which is scaled to body proportions. They are very sweet and petite but they don't like to be called so. They are full of life and enjoy having fun.

Alright men, you can join me again!

Like it or not, people do judge a book by its cover. Do you dress to impress other people? Are you constantly trying to attract the attention of the opposite sex? Do you dress so that no one will notice you? Do you purely dress for comfort without regard to appearance? Do you dress for yourself? Do you grab the daily sweat pants and not really care?

I firmly believe that you teach people how to treat you based on how you dress. What you wear does not define you as a person, but what you wear is a reflection of how you feel about yourself. Re-read that.

Author of <u>Dress for Success</u>, John T. Malloy conducted a very interesting experiment in the Port Authority Bus Terminal and Grand Central Station in New York City. His research involved stopping people to say that he was terribly embarrassed, but he had left his wallet at home and needed 75 cents to get home. He carried this experiment on for two hours during the rush hour. During the first hour, he wore a suit without a tie; for the second hour, he wore the same suit, but added a neck tie.

In the first hour, he made $7.23, but in the second hour with his tie on, he made $26.00. He concluded, "No question then: The tie is a symbol of respectability and responsibility; it communicates to other people who you are, or reinforces or detracts from their conception of who you should be."

After researching and conducting thousands of studies, experiments, and tests over a period of years, Mr. Molloy concludes that what a person wears is directly related to the success he will have in life. "We all wear uniforms and our uniforms are clear and distinct signs of class. We react to them accordingly."

Clothes do say something about you. They openly reveal your attitudes toward yourself (self-image and self-esteem), toward others (the people you attract), toward your work (its importance), and toward God (your reverence or lack of reverence toward Him).

I want you to dress in a way that makes you feel good about you, about your emotional wholeness and your promising new future.

I remember in college during some of my communication classes, we were told these tips on colors that I think are just fun and interesting: (from Color Psychology—Infoplease.com)

Black: the color of authority and power. It is used excessively in fashion because it makes people appear thinner. It is also stylish and timeless. Black also implies submission. Priests wear black to signify submission to God. Some fashion experts say a woman wearing black implies submission to men. Black outfits can also be overpowering, or make the wearer seem aloof or evil. Villains, such as Dracula, often wear black.

White: Brides wear white to symbolize innocence and purity. White reflects light and is considered a summer color. White is popular in decorating and in fashion because it is light, neutral, and goes with everything. Doctors and nurses wear white to imply sterility.

Red: The most emotionally intense color, red stimulates a faster heartbeat and breathing. It is also the color of love. Red clothing gets noticed and makes the wearer appear heavier. Since it is an extreme color, red clothing might not help people in negotiations or confrontations. Red cars are popular targets for thieves. In decorating, red is usually used as an accent. Decorators say that red furniture should be perfect since it will attract attention.

Pink: The most romantic color, pink, is more tranquilizing. Sports teams sometimes paint the locker rooms used by opposing teams bright pink so their opponents will lose energy.

Blue: The color of the sky and the ocean, blue is one of the most popular colors. It causes the opposite reaction as red. Peaceful, tranquil blue causes the body to produce calming chemicals, so it is often used in bedrooms. Blue can also be cold and depressing. Fashion consultants recommend wearing blue to job interviews because it symbolizes loyalty. People are more productive in blue rooms. Studies show weightlifters are able to handle heavier weights in blue gyms.

Green: Green symbolizes nature. It is the easiest color on the eye and can improve vision. It is a calming, refreshing color. People waiting to appear on TV sit in "green rooms" to relax. Hospitals often use green because it relaxes patients. Brides in the Middle Ages wore green to symbolize fertility. Dark green is masculine, conservative, and implies wealth.

Yellow: Cheerful sunny yellow is an attention getter. While it is considered an optimistic color, people lose their tempers more often in yellow rooms, and babies will cry more. It is the most difficult color for the eye to take in, so it can be overpowering if overused. Yellow enhances concentration, hence its use for legal pads. It also speeds metabolism.

Purple: The color of royalty, purple connotes luxury, wealth, and sophistication. It is also feminine and romantic. However, because it is rare in nature, purple can appear artificial.

Brown: Solid, reliable brown is the color of earth and is abundant in nature. Light brown implies genuineness while dark brown is similar to wood or leather. Brown can also be sad and wistful. Men are more apt to say brown is one of their favorite colors.

Black: People who choose black as their favorite color are often artistic and sensitive. While these people aren't introverts, they are careful with the details of their lives and do not share easily with others.

White: People who like white are often organized and logical and don't have a great deal of clutter in their lives.

Red: Those who love red live life to the fullest and are tenacious and determined in their endeavors.

Blue: If blue is your favorite color you love harmony, are reliable, sensitive and always make an effort to think of others. You like to keep thinks clean and tidy and feel that stability is the most important aspect in life.

Green: Those who love the color green are often affectionate, loyal and frank. Green lovers are also aware of what others think of them and consider their reputation very important.

Yellow: You enjoy learning and sharing your knowledge with others. Finding happiness comes easy to you and others would compare you to sunshine.

Purple: You are artistic and unique. You have a great respect for people but at times can be arrogant.

Brown: You are a good friend and try your hardest to be reliable and dependable. Flashy objects are not something you desire; you just want a stable life.

Isn't it interesting that even the colors we choose to wear are communicting a message? So what does the color say about you?

This information is meant to be fun and informative, not a cut and dry evaluation of your life from head to toe. So, just enjoy the colors and have fun wearing whatever you're attracted to each day.

(The Color Test Published on June 6, 2011 by Bernardo Tirado, PMP in Digital Leaders).

It's a fact: Looking bad makes us feel bad.

Have you ever noticed how you look when you're physically sick? Next time you visit a doctor's office, notice the people in the waiting room chairs. Less than attractive, right? They haven't showered or brushed their bedhead, and they are wearing baggy sweat pants and a pajama shirt! I know we are dealing with emotional sickness in this book, not physical sickness; however, many wounded souls have also neglected their physical appearance during their suffering.

The way we dress communicates a picture of our self worth. What we wear profoundly affects the way we feel. Many wounded souls are showing it in the way they dress and in the way they carry themselves.

There are times in the Bible when Jesus healed people, they instantly got a new image of themselves *inside and out.*

In Mark 10:46-52 (*NLT*), we read the story of a man called Blind Bartimaeus. Back in that era, if one were blind, they assumed the position as a beggar and beggars wore certain clothes that associated them with their lifestyle.

> Then they reached Jericho, and as Jesus and his disciples left town, a large crowd followed him. A blind beggar named Bartimaeus (son of Timaeus) was sitting beside the road. When Bartimaeus heard that Jesus of Nazareth was nearby, he began to shout, "Jesus, Son of David, have mercy on me!"
>
> "Be quiet!" many of the people yelled at him.
>
> But he only shouted louder, "Son of David, have mercy on me!"
>
> When Jesus heard him, he stopped and said, "Tell him to come here."
>
> So they called the blind man. "Cheer up," they said. "Come on, he's calling you!"
>
> Bartimaeus threw aside his coat, jumped up, and came to Jesus.
>
> "What do you want me to do for you?" Jesus asked.
>
> "My rabbi," the blind man said, "I want to see!"

And Jesus said to him, "Go, for your faith has healed you." Instantly the man could see, and he followed Jesus down the road.

You could say, he laid aside his beggarly clothes. Why? Those clothes represent his old life—the life of a beggar, an outcast, his past. It's time to throw away those beggarly clothes!

A new look can help give you a new attitude about your future.

In no way am I advising that you invest in a whole new wardrobe, trust me, I know how expensive that can be. I am a bargain-shopper and proud of it! However, I am saying that changing a few things in your appearance can have a profound affect on how you feel inside.

Take a shower.

Get a new hairstyle.

Shave.

Put some cologne or perfume on.

Add a little more mascara.

Add a scarf to that T-shirt and jeans.

Put some earrings on and pull your hair back.

Buy a new piece of clothing.

I want you to learn to love yourself. Feel good about yourself. Take care of yourself. Respect yourself. Do something different physically such as taking a walk for 20 minutes a day.

There is a direct link between physical health and emotional health. Proverbs 14:30 says, "A sound heart is life to the body" (*NKJV*).

Your mind and your emotions are greatly affected by the condition of your body. Some doctors agree that many emotional problems can be controlled through good physical health. I recommend that you go to a doctor to have regular check-ups. Taking care of your body affects every aspect of your life.

Walking outside or on a treadmill during bad weather days has become a part of my daily routine and has produced significant changes in my body and my emotional health. There's just something about walking outside in the fresh air that brings peace. Fitness experts advise walking outside regularly because it is the greatest exercise you can do for your body, mind and emotions.

I can't tell you enough how important it is for your overall wellbeing that you do some kind of exercise. Years ago, I determined to walk for 30 minutes everyday for 21 days consistently. I knew that if I could do something consistently for 21 days, I could break an old habit and start a new one. That was in 2001, and I haven't stopped since. Change your habits, and you'll change your future.

I want you to get a new image of yourself as beautiful, healthy and whole, someone with a divine calling on their lives, someone who cares about themselves. I'm not saying you have to become a bodybuilder or a fitness expert, nor am I saying that you need to get all dressed up every day. I'm not saying you have to wear as much mascara as I do. I want you to do what you need to do to feel better about yourself. And carry yourself as someone with dignity, someone that Jesus died for specifically.

As a confident person, you should always pull your shoulders back (consciously work on your posture), hold your head up, maintain firm eye contact with whomever you're communicating, and give firm handshakes and smile.

Laugh again.

Proverbs 17:22 says, "A cheerful heart is good medicine, but a broken spirit saps a person's strength"

Joy is contagious.

(*NLT*). It has been proven medically that laugher heals wounds. If you laugh on a regular basis, you tend to make better decisions.

Norman Cousins, one time editor of the *Saturday Review*, found himself very ill at one time in his life. He was diagnosed with a connective tissue disorder after a trip to Russia in 1964. Thinking his illness could be stress related, Norman decided to purposely bring more joy and laughter into his life.

While he was in the hospital, he would watch videos of *The Three Stooges* repeatedly. As he watched these slapstick routines, he would laugh and laugh and laugh. Eventually, he began to feel better. He used laughter to boost his immune system, which in turn gave him the strength needed to fight his illness. His severe symptoms went away and he went back to his normal life.

There is healing power in laughter. God is the One who came up with this medicine. The next time you turn on the TV and surf the channels, make a conscious effort to stop on a channel with a (clean) show that will make you laugh. Read humorous books and jokes that even make you just smile.

"A sound heart is life to the body" (Prov. 14:30, *NKJV*).

Have you ever walked into a house

where people had been fighting? You can just feel the awkwardness in the atmosphere. When people are constantly sad, uneasy, pessimistic, or moody, it leaves an "odor" that spreads throughout the atmosphere, but so does joy and laughter.

When you are cheerful around other people, even if you are feeling down, they respond cheerfully. Your cheerfulness, makes them have a cheerful attitude around you. Joel Osteen says, "Happiness breeds happiness."

Have you ever overheard someone laughing really hard, and even though you don't know why they are laughing, you start to laugh? Their laughter rubbed off on you. Joy is contagious. Laughing helps to bring about inner healing.

How many times do you laugh each day? Research has shown that kids laugh up to 400 times a day leave it for no reason. That's the important part: for no reason. They just find life funny, or maybe they find themselves funny. They laugh at anything and every thing.

How many times do we tell kids to stop it, tone it down, be quiet? Eventually, they have it engrained in them to be like us. Research showed adults laugh 15 times a day *at most*. What happened to 400?

Nehemiah 8:10 says, "The joy of the Lord is your strength" (*NKJV*).

Joy will give you strength. For what? Everything.

If you are what you wear, then wear a smile, wear confidence, wear class, wear whatever makes you feel your best.

"I decided I need to break free"

"I just recently got out from a wrong relationship, a bad soul tie. For more than three years, Satan took a hold of me. The Lord gave me a way out many times, but I always ignored Him. Finally, God showed me a man – a missionary with a servant's heart. He is so close to the Lord. I thought to myself, "Oh, this is my dream guy, this is the man I've been praying for all my life!" I began thinking about what I've got myself into with this bad soul tie. "Why do I have a boyfriend who's heart is far from God, why did I allow myself to have sex before marriage over and over again?" I decided I need to break free. I'm currently in the process of seeking the Lord and I believe it's not an accident that I saw your podcasts. It really has helped me. I confess that God's plan for me is to prosper me and give me hope in the future. Thank you so much. Please pray that God will use me mightily for his glory. God bless."

- Lhevie

Chapter 13

Boost Your Self-Image

When I was in college taking a Psychology class, the professor asked each of us to get out a sheet of paper and draw a picture of the way we see ourselves. Everyone had to do this. So, I began by drawing my round head, and then added gigantic, bulging frog eyes that took up the whole face (with long eyelashes, of-course!) The nose and lips weren't that big of a focus. As I began to draw the body, I drew bony, emaciated-looking arms and wrists but massive, huge thighs that covered each side of the paper! With my knees being what we call "knock-kneed" I drew my legs almost looking like a contortionist going inward toward each other. Then I grabbed a red pen and started just putting dots all over the drawing. The guy next to me said, "Are you OK?" I said, "Uh-huh. Just fine." He said, "What's all that?" I said, "My freckles!" And I hammered away. When I held the drawing up, I looked a little bit like a freak. Which was the professor's point exactly: your self-image may be distorted.

> You behave in a manner consistent with how you see yourself.

What is your *self-image*? *Your self image is simply a portrait you carry around of yourself.* It's how you see yourself and how you think others see you.

Just like those distorted mirrors at the amusement parks, Satan loves to distort the truth and convince you to believe it. From the moment you are born, he works overtime to try to convince you that you are unloved, unwanted, insignificant, fat, ugly, deformed, crazy, and worthless. He wants your self-image distorted. Why? *Because if you have a poor self-image, you'll never be confident enough to do what God put you on this earth to do.*

According to the National Institute of Mental Health, approximately one in four Americans are diagnosed each year with a psychological disorder, the majority for which low self-esteem and a poor self-image are underlying factors.

The truth is that once you've accepted a poor identity—once that poor self-image is accepted—you make choices that support your beliefs about yourself. Your self-image can be seen in the way you dress, the way you talk about yourself, the relationships you choose, your career, your relationship with God. Every area of your life is affected by your self-image.

You behave in a manner consistent with how you see yourself.

If you see yourself as having no value and no worth, then you'll make decisions that agree with that sense of no self-worth.

I read a story about a guy named Victor who, at 15 years old, was told by his teacher that he wouldn't amount to much and that he should drop out of school and learn a trade. Because he was told he was an idiot, he acted like one for the next 17 years. Then, when he was 32 years old, he found out he had an IQ of 161. Since discovering how smart he really was, he has written books, secured several patents, become a successful businessman and chairman of the Mensa Society, which has the qualification of an IQ of 140 or higher.

Reasons for poor self-image:
- Words spoken over you (by parents, teachers, coaches, peers, boyfriends/girlfriends, spouses)
- Abandonment by parents or spouse
- Divorce
- Abuse (physical, verbal, sexual, emotional)
- Rejection
- Comparison to a sibling
- Turmoil in the home
- Marriage rejection, unfaithfulness
- Rape
- Being made fun of or talked down to

and the list goes on…

Satan will use whatever situation he can to in-still a poor sense of self-worth. Why? If you don't value yourself, no one else will either.

> Only the Word of God can change a poor self-image into the image of God.

When I was a youth pastor, I invited all the teenage girls over to my house one night to talk to them about their self-image. I held up this fresh, cold Coke drizzling with ice and asked, "Who wants the first sip?" Everyone raised their hands. "I do. I want the first sip." I gave it to one girl and she took a big gulp. Then, I said, "Pass it to your best friend." She took a sip. Then, she passed it to her friend. About five girls later, I got the Coke back and noticed there was about one drink left. I said, "OK. Who wants the last little sip?" They all yelled, "That's disgusting. It's backwash!" Nobody wanted the left over.

I said, "Many times we see ourselves like this Coke can. We've been passed around from guy to guy, from relationship to relationship, from abuse to abuse. We feel used up, washed up, like nobody wants us, as if we've lost all our value and worth. What do we have to offer anyone?"

The point was well-taken. We assume we're not valuable because of the experiences of our past, so we behave in a manner consistent with how we see ourselves. We dress that way. We act that way. We talk that way. We choose friends who agree with our negative opinion of ourselves. And we don't expect God to really bless us or use us in a meaningful way.

You believe yourself more than anyone.

If you have low self-esteem, it doesn't matter what anyone else says to you, how many compliments you receive, awards you are given or church services you attend. If you don't believe in yourself, you'll never change.

T.D. Jakes says, "You can't take a person who feels ugly about themselves and make them feel lovely." He said, "They cannot retain the encouragement because they are leaking from the inside. Only the Word of God will get down on the inside of your soul and fix the plumbing so you can retain what God has placed in you." Only the Word of God can change a poor self-image into the image of God.

Do you realize that Satan has a plan to stop you from the plan of God for your life? It's not haphazard or coincidental. It's strategic and on purpose. Why? Because he does not want you to fulfill God's plan for your life.

"Before I made you in your mother's womb, I chose you. Before you were born, *I set you apart for a special work.*" (Jer. 1:5, *NCV*, emphasis added).

God needs you. He wants to use you. He has a special plan and purpose, an assignment, for you to fulfill during your time on Earth. You don't have time to waste. Maybe you've been abused, and never told anyone. Maybe you were wounded, rejected, abandoned, or violated. Maybe you're consumed with guilt over your past: you had sex before marriage, you got pregnant, you had an abortion, and you let yourself down. Don't let Satan paint a picture in your mind of who you were back then. If you've repented of your mistakes, then you've been made a new creation in Christ Jesus. Old things have passed away and all things have become new—including your self-image (2 Cor. 5:17).

"May you stay in one place forever!"

I was reading a story about a tribe from Asia who would yell curses at their enemies. The worst curses that they could possibly think of were not, "May your swords rust and you die of a disease!" Instead, they would yell, "May you stay in one place forever!"

That's exactly what Satan is yelling in your mind. May you stay in one place for the rest of your life! He wants you to stay locked in those memories of that wrong soul tie forever. He wants you tormented with the pain permanently. He wants you to think that you will never get over this. He wants you to relive an experience of rejection, abuse, violation, intimidation forever. Why? Because ultimately, it distorts your self-image crippling you from ever doing what God wants you to do with your life. I speak from experience.

Because of the different things I've been through in my life, I had such a poor self-image, very insecure and inferior, and it didn't matter what my parents told me, how popular I was in school or how many sermons I heard at church, I saw myself a certain way and that was final in my mind. It wasn't until I began to fill my mind, I mean taking drastic steps to fill my mind, with God's love for me, that I began to change from the inside out.

General Douglass McArthur said one of the most important rules of war is to know your enemy. You need to know, first of all, who you are fighting. Satan. He's the thief who has stolen your identity and distorted your self-image.

Your war is with the devil. Remember that. Remind yourself of this fact often. Your war is not with that soul tie—it's with the enemy of your soul, Satan. He is the one you are fighting—not that individual.

You can't stay mad at the people who hurt you for the rest of your life. You have to get mad at the right enemy or else you're in a losing battle. Once you've discovered that Satan is the one behind every touch of evil in your life then you can target all of your pain towards him. How? Get on a quest to know God more intimately than you ever have before. Why is that? Because God's love will drive fear, right out of your life.

Chosen by God

Isaiah 41:9 means so much to me. It clearly says, "I have chosen you and have not cast you away" (*NKJV*). I want you to think about that verse applying directly to you. God has chosen you—no matter what you've done, no matter what has been done to you—and He has not and will not cast you away. That's a good scripture for you to memorize and confess out of your mouth every time Satan puts insecure thoughts in your mind.

"God has chosen me and has not cast me away." In other words, you are the perfect person for the job, the promotion, the marriage, the family, the dreams that are in your heart.

You might be thinking:

But my husband cheated on me... "I have chosen you and have not cast you away."

But my dad abused me... "I have chosen you and have not cast you away."

But I was raped and rejected... "I have chosen you and have not cast you away."

But I was dumped by someone I loved... "I have chosen you and have not cast you away."

But I did some awful things... "I have chosen you and have not cast you away."

But I've really made some huge mistakes in my life... "I have chosen you and have not cast you away."

In order for you to fulfill your life assignment or to do what God has put you on this earth to do, it will absolutely require that you know that God has chosen you—no matter what. And I have discovered that God chooses the least likely people to do the most amazing things through. Look at some of the flaws listed in Rick Warren's book <u>The Purpose Driven Life</u> from the people God hand-picked to use in a powerful way:

Abraham was old.

Jacob was insecure.

Leah was unattractive.

Joseph was abused.

Moses stuttered.

Gideon was poor.

Samson was codependent.

Rahab was immoral.

David had an affair and all kinds of family problems.

Elijah was suicidal.

Jeremiah was depressed.

Jonah was reluctant.

Naomi was a widow.

John the Baptist was eccentric to say the least.

Peter was impulsive and hot-tempered.

Martha worried a lot.

The Samaritan woman had several failed marriages.

Zaccheus was unpopular.

Thomas had doubts.

Paul had poor health.

Timothy was timid.

Misfits. But God used each of them in His service. He will use you, too, if you stop making excuses.

I don't know about you, but I can relate to many of those misfits. At the same time, if God can use them then why can't He use you? Why can't you go after those dreams that are in your heart that seem so impossible right now?

Jeremiah 1:5 says, "Before I made you in your mother's womb, I chose you. Before you were born, I set you apart for a special work" (*NCV*).

God has a special work for you to accomplish during your time here on Earth and He is fully expecting you to carry it out. However, you must have a positive self image if you're ever going to fully carry out your assignment.

Andrew Carnegie said, "Men are developed the same way gold is mined. When gold is mined, several tons of dirt must be moved to get an ounce of gold, but one doesn't go into the mine looking for dirt. One goes in looking for gold."

I believe you are more valuable than an ounce of gold. God sees your potential. You need to see your potential. God sees what others don't see.

> If you see yourself as forgiven, loved, valuable, confident, chosen—you are.

A Matter of the Heart

In 1 Samuel 16, God was prepared to anoint David to be the next King. David's dad, Jesse, brought all of his sons in to be chosen except David. Right away Satan was trying to belittle David and make him feel insecure in the fact that they wouldn't even consider him as a possibility. But God saw what other people didn't see.

They brought the oldest son who was big and powerful and said, "Surely the Lord has anointed him."

"But the Lord said to Samuel, Look not on his appearance or at the height of his stature, for I have rejected him. *For the Lord sees not as man sees; for man looks on the outward appearance, but the Lord looks on the heart*"(1 Sam. 16:7, *AMP*, emphasis added).

I want you to know that God is truly looking on your heart. You may have messed up pretty badly in the past and Satan has convinced you that you could never be used of God now. He told me the same lies. He still tells me those lies—that's why stories like David's are so encouraging. God chooses the least likely. God is not looking at your performance once you've repented; He is looking at the condition of your heart. He forgives you. He's not mad at you. He's not punishing you. He wants to use you.

Your Life is not a Waste

God knows that you will never fulfill your destiny if you never see yourself chosen. If you continue to wallow around in all of your mistakes and continue replaying all those negative words that have been spoken over you, His hands are tied.

I love the story in John 6:12 where Jesus instructed the disciples to "gather up the fragments that nothing be wasted." You may think that your past was nothing but a fragmented waste. All those years were wasted. Your childhood was wasted. Your marriage was a waste. That relationship was a big waste. God is saying, "gather up the fragments that remain, that *nothing* be lost" (John 6:12, *KJV* emphasis added). He chose you with your past, your weaknesses, your temptations, your struggles. Why? He wants to use them.

Rick Warren says, "Other people are going to find healing in your wounds. Your greatest life message and your most effective ministry will come out of your deepest hurts. The things you're most embarrassed about, most ashamed of, and most reluctant to share are the very tools God can use most powerfully to heal others."

It's imperative that you improve your self-image in two ways:

1. Change the way you think about yourself.
2. Change the way you speak about yourself.

Nothing will change in your life until you begin thinking differently. Proverbs 23:7 says, "For as he thinks in his heart, so is he" (*NKJV*). If you see yourself as a loser, you are. If you see yourself as insignificant, you are. If you see yourself as trashy, worthless, crazy, psycho, messed up, used up—you are. But if you see yourself as forgiven, loved, valuable, confident, chosen—you are.

Norman Vincent Peale tells a story about a tattoo parlor in China where American sailors would get tattoos. He noticed a tattoo displayed in the window that he couldn't believe anyone would really get. It read, "Born to Lose". He walked inside to ask the tattoo artist if people really got that tattoo. In broken English, the Chinese man replied, "Before tattooed on body, tattooed on mind."

Well, how do you change the way you've thought for 10, 20, 30 years? Romans 12:2 says, "Be transformed by the renewing of your mind" (*NKJV*). What do you renew your mind to? The Word of God. We settled that in Chapter 7.

Renewing your mind is a two-step process. It's getting rid of the old way of thinking and replacing with a new way of thinking about yourself. What you desperately need more than anything is to hear the Word consistently.

If your mind is tormented with fearful, insecure, debilitating thoughts, then you're not hearing enough Word. If you lay down at night and your mind is racing with hopelessness, fear, anxiety, painful memories, then you need to get a plan to hear the Word more today than you did yesterday. You need to "kick it up a notch higher," so to speak.

You need to begin speaking differently about yourself. It doesn't matter if you have been told, "She's the wild one." "She's the quitter." "She's sleazy." "He's crazy." "He's a loser." "She's prone to making bad choices." "She's a failure."

God's Word is final authority!

You need to decide whose words have more power over you. Some person's? Or God's? And stop agreeing with the devil.

How do you begin to change the way you speak? Stop putting yourself down. You may think it, but don't say it.

Never again say, "I'm fat." "I'm ugly." "I'm a loser." Do not let those damaging words come out of your mouth. Your words have a powerful way of keeping you trapped to the very thing you are speaking.

Four steps to feel better about yourself

1. Accept compliments.

Simply practice saying, "Thank you." If someone says, "You look so pretty." Do not reply with, "You've got to be kidding me! I look terrible." Just say, "Thank you." And go on. Stop refusing compliments with complaints about what you don't like. Confident people accept and enjoy being complimented. Practice it today.

2. Speak positive declarations over yourself.

What you repeatedly hear, you eventually believe. I made a list of positive affirmations that I have been speaking over myself consistently since 2007. Do you know what? I am not the girl I used to be. God has truly transformed my self-image. You could speak things such as:

I am confident and courageous.
I am disciplined, spirit, soul and body.
I am highly focused.
I am creative.
I am on time.
I am highly favored with God and man.
I am beautiful inside and out.
I am healthy.
I am wealthy.
I am a giver.
I am successful.

I hear God's voice clearly.

Make a list of how you would love to be described and begin saying it.

3. Speak God's Word over yourself.

Yes, you will feel silly the first time you do this, but it works. I promise you. Every time rejection tries to consume your mind and prevent you from stepping out, speak this verse out loud:

> "*I have chosen you* and not cast you off. Fear not, for *I am with you*; do not look around you in terror and be dismayed, for I am your God. I will strengthen and harden you to difficulties, yes, I will help you; yes, I will hold you up and retain you with My right hand of rightness and justice" (Isa. 41:9-10, *AMP*, emphasis added).

4. Do it consistently.

You can't do something three or four times and expect to see change. Make it a part of your daily routine. Before you head out the door for work, go in another room and just speak your confessions out loud. I am writing from experience, you will change the way you see yourself.

Remember consistency is the key to change in every area of your life. As you consistently hear the Word and speak the Word over yourself, your self-image will be completely transformed, and your self-image affects your entire destiny. If God can use me, the least likely, He can use you too.

Restore the years.

According to Joel 2:25, God can even restore the years that Satan stole from you. Don't ever think of your life as a waste or a regret. Use it. Use your pain to help someone else. That's why I'm even writing this book. The broken become masters at mending.

"All God's giants were weak people."
- Hudson Taylor

God specializes in turning our weaknesses into strengths. All those things you hate about yourself right now, God wants to use. I want you to get a vision to use your pain to help somebody else.

You have vision on the inside of you. There's so much for you to enjoy in life. Start making a list of things to do, places to see, people to meet, accomplishes to pursue.

- Go see Washington D.C. and tour the White House
- Go to Venice, Italy, take a boat ride in the Gondolas
- Go to the top of the Eiffel Tower
- Volunteer at a homeless shelter
- Go on a mission trip to Africa, Haiti, India, etc.
- Save $5,000
- Ride a horse on the beach
- Take a cooking class
- Make a scrapbook for your children
- Take flying lessons
- Learn to speak a foreign language
- Weigh your perfect weight
- Color your hair
- Participate in a marathon
- Paint your bedroom
- Read a new book each month for a year

· Get a pedicure

Dream again. It brings life—it brings healing. Remember, your life isn't over because that relationship is. This is just the beginning of what God wants to do in your life. Begin your routine that will lead you to your dreams.

> Consistency is the key to change in every area of your life.

"God had something greater for me"

"I want to share a testimony with you thanks to your series on soul ties. I have overcome so many things in my life and truly desire to live my life for the Lord.

But there was one thing that was my cryptonite...my first "love" from high school. He could contact me and I would let my guard down so easily. I was in love with him at 16 and he's kept in touch every so often every year since then. I just couldn't figure out why there was this attachment, why with all of my power and prayer I could not erase these feelings. He's since married these past 3 years and continued to contact me and tell me how much he "loved" me. I went through a serious emotional breakdown 2 years ago, which included 3 days of fasting in order to get me out of this situation of feeling so attached to him. I changed my phone number, blocked all his emails and instant messages...I ran from sin!

Then we were in contact again (via Facebook). I ran away from sin again by not responding to his messages. I met with a Christian friend and she told me about soul ties. I had never ever heard of soul ties so I looked it up online to see if this lined up with the·Word. Then I found your YouTube series on soul ties. Prior to watching this I said, "Lord you have to be gentle with me, please give me an answer of what I should do, but please be gentle." Your message was done in such a loving way, and was scripture based, and I felt it was OK to lift those scriptures up to the Lord and get ready to remove this obstacle in my life. I'm telling you the minute I lifted those scriptures and those words to break this soul tie to the Lord, was the minute He broke that tie.

I am 30, and have struggled with this for 14 years. I have desired a Christian husband ever since I was a little girl. And that was the original reason I had broken up with my "first love". I knew God had something greater for me. I honestly feel that I wouldn't have been ready for what God has in store for me had I not prayed for God to break this tie in my life. I just want to thank you and encourage you to keep speaking the Word of God in love to people. You never know who is watching and how many generations and lives you will impact.

The ex-boyfriend contacted me recently through Facebook and I was able to delete the message without blinking, without any feeling WHATSOEVER...that is truly the work of God.

My future thanks you and I thank God that I know you...online! Since watching your videos our lives have never been the same. Keep up the good work!"

- Alanna

Terri Savelle Foy

For years, Terri Savelle Foy's life was average. She had no dreams to pursue. Each passing day was just a repeat of the day before. Finally, with a marriage in trouble and her life falling apart, Terri made a change. She began to pursue God like never before, develop a new routine and discovered the power of having a dream and purpose.

As Terri started to recognize her own dreams and goals, she simply wrote them down and reviewed them consistently. This written vision became a road map to drive her life. As a result, those dreams are now a reality.

Terri has become the Founder of an international Christian ministry. She is the host of the Live Your Dreams television broadcast, an author, a conference speaker, and a success coach to hundreds of thousands of people all over the world. Her best-selling books Make Your Dreams Bigger than Your Memories, Imagine Big, and Pep Talk have helped people discover how to overcome the hurts of the past and see the possibilities of a limitless future. Her weekly podcast is a lifeline of hope and inspiration to people around the world.

Terri Savelle Foy is a cheerleader of dreams and is convinced that "if you can dream it, God can do it." She is known across the globe as a world-class motivator of hope and success through her transparent and humorous teaching style. Terri's unique ability to communicate success strategies in a simple and practical way has awakened the dreams of the young and old alike.

Terri shares from personal experience the biblical concepts of using the gift of the imagination to reach full potential in Jesus Christ. From stay-at-home moms to business executives, Terri consistently inspires others to go after their dreams. With step-by-step instruction and the inspiration to follow through, people are fueled with the passion to complete their life assignment down to the last detail (see John 17:4).

Terri and her husband, Rodney Foy, have been married since 1991, and are the parents of a beautiful redheaded daughter, Kassidi Cherie. They live near Dallas, Texas. For more information about Terri, go to *www.terri.com*.